Sampa HAY
st. Jus
10/14

- 4 APR 2015

Wade.

1 7 JAN 2019

7 FEB 2019

From 28 FEB 2019

in Camb

24 HOUR RENEWAL HOTLINE 0845 607 6119

www.cornwall.gov.uk/library

one and all · onen hag oll

First published April 2012
by Kenwater Books, Kenwater House,
Green Lane, Leominster, Herefordshire HR6 8QJ

kenwaterbooks@gmail.com

Cover design: Nicholas Lewis

ISBN 978-0-9571832-0-9

Set in 12pt Baskerville and printed in England by Orphans Press Ltd.,
Arrow Close, Leominster Enterpise Park, Leominster, Herefordshire HR6 0LD.

CONTENTS

ILLUSTRATIONS

This book is dedicated to
Fritz's great-grandchildren
and his great-great-grandchildren
with whom he would have been
so delighted

Alex
Matthew Joe
Ben   Pete Mike Nick
Elizabeth   David
Katharine Olivia
Alexandra

Adrien
Manon Finley
Eddie Louis Alice Rose
Bethany Sam Tom Pattie
Freddie   Gwen
Lucien Emily
Archie

ACKNOWLEDGEMENTS

I am indebted to a large number of people for the care with which they answered my questions, and in many cases the degree to which they volunteered new material. The library staff at the National Maritime Museum in Falmouth were enthusiastic from the early stages of the project and enabled me to talk to David Wilson (author of *Falmouth Haven*) and Roger Stevens who helped to identify quay punts and Falmouth working boats. Steve Jenkins at the Cornish Studies Library in Redruth helped with research and Elizabeth le Grice dug out documents on the Falmouth Waterworks and plans for sewage disposal. The late Brian Stewart, when he was Director of the Falmouth Art Gallery, was hugely enthusiastic and provided, among other things, some of the less well-known information on Cornish artists, and Margaret Powell from Lamorna shared her extensive knowledge of the Freeman and Hemy families. Lee Mitchell, Sexton of Falmouth Town Cemetery, carried out an extraordinary piece of detective work in finding family graves, some of which were completely unmarked.

Archivists are a special breed and I am indebted to Charlotte Bleasdale in New Zealand for shipping data from John Swire and Company, Geraldine O'Driscoll at the Royal College of Surgeons, Dr Robin Darwall-Smith at Magdalen College, Oxford, and James Cox and Eleanor Harding at Gonville and Caius College, Cambridge, also Sue Small, Librarian of the China and East Asia Section at the School of Oriental and African Studies Library

From the world of publishing, I am grateful to Ian Grant of Cornwall Editions Limited and Professor Philip Payton, the author, for permission to quote from *The Cornish Overseas*. Also to Jerry Johns of Polperro Heritage Press who offered much encouragement and invaluable advice and Geoff Swallow from St Ives who shared some of his research into the annual swimming matches in the Southwest and traced references to Fritz at St Ives. Thanks also to David Tovey for the image of W H Bartlett's painting of the start of a swimming race at St Ives.

Most of the photographs and figures are reproduced with permission from private collections and although every effort has been made to trace the source of all the illustrations there may be unintentional omissions, which the publishers sincerely regret and will be glad to make amends in any future edition.

Andy Bowden, Gary Nozedar and Duncan Betts at Orphans Press in Leominster were outstanding in giving advice and support as well as doing a superb printing job. Martin Bates compiled the index and has given meticulous advice on the text, but any mistakes or ambiguities remain the responsibility of the author. In particular there was a problem with finding a systematic format for Chinese proper names given that printed sources often contained variations even within a single publication, quite apart from Fritz's own preferences that varied in different volumes of his diaries! The intention has been to remain faithful to the original sources and hopefully avoid giving any offence.

My cousin Penny Beamont has been continually supportive and managed to extract some key military information from the authorities about her father Jim Lewis, as well as providing other background information.

I am particularly indebted to my sons, Mike who read an early draft and Nick who designed the cover, but especially to my wife Sara who not only read drafts but continued to be encouraging even during my most obsessive phases.

Richard Lewis

INTRODUCTION

Among my mother's possessions were eleven very small diaries that had belonged to my grandfather and spanned the years 1905 to 1928. Although there was less than two inches of space per day, he managed to capture the essence of what was happening around him, as well as keeping a precise record of every single penny and cent that he spent. At first reading the diaries appeared to be just a factual record kept for personal reasons, but gradually they started to come alive as a picture of what life was like in China at the beginning of the last century, and then for a family in Cornwall through the First World War and the years of the Depression. The thread that runs through the narrative is the relationship between my grandfather and the woman he loved who was a member of the Freeman family who nurtured the Cornish granite industry through the nineteenth and into the twentieth century.

In order to earn enough money to marry his fiancée Fritz travelled to China to work as a marine engineer and found a country that was threatened on all sides both politically and economically. Returning to Cornwall as a slightly richer but very much wiser man, he found himself in another country that was struggling to rediscover itself in the aftermath of having been a world leader in the production of copper and tin, with the same uncertainty at that stage about what the future might hold.

Fritz's story is a glimpse through a window in time at global changes that were taking place a hundred years ago and are reflected in what we see today in the first quarter of the present century.

Richard Lewis

PART ONE

NORWAY

Chapter 1

FJORD to FAL

January in Norway is always cold, but the winter of 1871 felt particularly bitter to Ellen Lewis as she prepared for the birth of her ninth child. The temperature in Christiania[1] had fallen to nearly thirty degrees below zero, causing the fjord to freeze over and described by one visitor as having become 'a perfect mass of giant columns of steam curling up from the water, as if the sea had been bewitched'.[2] Ellen suffered from asthma, and as a young bride she was brought to Norway by her husband, an English doctor, who was sure that the clear air and proximity to the sea would help her breathing and be good for her health. Arthur was however a typical Victorian husband and did not appear to consider that ten pregnancies in twenty years would be other than a moderate norm for his wife, though it does say something for her fortitude, and perhaps his skill as a doctor, that nine of her children survived to adulthood.

Fritz was born on the 14th January 1872 at Holte, in East Bærum, on the western edge of Christiania, and he differed from

[1] Present day Oslo

[2] Beauclerk, *Summer and Winter in Norway*, p.105.

1

Ellen Lewis, Fritz's mother,   Dr Arthur Lewis
in Oslo in 1873

the rest of his family in being given a Scandinavian rather than an English first name. Joseph was the eldest child, followed at regular intervals by Ernest, Harold, Charles and Walter, with Kate being in the middle as the only surviving girl at that stage, before Norah arrived in 1870, to be followed by Fritz, and ultimately Ralph.

There are no surviving records for this period of the Lewis family's life, apart from the stories passed down through the generations and happily repeated by Fritz's wife, May, to her children and grandchildren. The tradition was that the boys were an unruly bunch and that Ellen generally despaired of trying to keep them in check, although that may have been more a reflection on her state of health and the fact that she was pregnant or nursing a baby most of the time. Arthur was described in the Norwegian census as a farmer rather than a doctor, but Fritz remembered patients coming to the house for consultations and leaving their horses and carriages outside. A favourite trick of the Lewis boys was to irritate the horses by tweaking hairs out of their tails and then asking the owners as they were leaving, to give them a horse tail hair as a memento. The innocent patient would tweak a hair from the horse's backside and frequently get kicked for their trouble, much to the amusement of the boys.

When Fritz was born his elder brothers were in their teens and Kate was old enough to help her mother with the younger children and the new baby. The special bond between Fritz and Kate was established at a very early age and it would have been easy for him to have become the ewe lamb in the flock and have been viewed by his boisterous brothers as tied to the women's apron strings. Fritz was however made of sterner stuff, and if there was a choice between a comfortably passive role and a more active independence, then he chose the latter with some determination. He was not physically big for his age, but what he lacked in volume he made up for in muscle, and was quickly recognized as the boy who would take risks and who would always rise to a challenge. In some ways he had the best of both worlds because he could challenge his elder brothers and often outwit them, but he could also find a doughty defender in Kate if he needed a refuge or simply someone to attend to passing injuries. As time went on the brothers tended to bond together in pairs but Fritz was the odd one out who learned how to make his own particular way in life, which would take him in due course on a journey from a very ordinary beginning on a small Norwegian farm, to Australia and later to China.

Fritz was born in the final quarter of the nineteenth century which turned out, in retrospect, to have been a time when large numbers of people around the world were on the move, searching for a better life than the one they were experiencing at home. Norwegians were emigrating to America to find space and freedom, while Cornwall, which would be where Fritz would grow up, was losing a large proportion of its young men to South America and Australia. Whole nations seemed to be in a melting pot and while some great powers declined, other relatively small countries surged forward to play important roles on the international stage. Strangely, Cornwall and China, which both played an important part in Fritz's story, were places which had experienced leading roles in the world, but whose power was in decline and seriously threatened from outside. The scale was of course dramatically different between the two, and while China led on a political stage, Cornwall's lead was in the world supply of copper, but the sense of being a victim and struggling to find a new role and respect in the world is remarkably similar in both countries in the late nineteenth and early twentieth centuries.

In global terms, it has been said that the nineteenth century was dominated by Great Britain as a major colonial power in the world, while the twentieth century was most influenced by America as it rose to prominence and exerted its influence in every corner of the globe. The jury is out as to which country will be most significant in the twenty-first century, but there is a feeling that it may be China. Whichever nation it turns out to be, the seeds of the future were being sown in the second half of the nineteenth century, and Fritz was a witness to that period in Britain, Australia and the Far East, and what he saw is reflected quite simply in the record of daily events which he kept in his diaries, as his attention was drawn more and more towards the Far East.

On the international stage, China was rapidly declining in power as imperial rule failed to grapple with the issues that surrounded its vast empire. European countries and America were determined to open up trade on China's south-western coast, while Russia was exerting pressure in Manchuria and the north-east. Japan had been hard at work developing its navy with the help of its ally Great Britain, and had inflicted damaging defeats on the weakening China. Russia was in trouble under Tzar Nicholas and its navy also suffered crushing defeats at the hands of the Japanese, rather too close in proximity to China for comfort. Britain was coming to the end of its colonial magnificence, and its maritime dominance was being challenged, particularly by America, which was rapidly rising as a world power, and was subtly spreading its influence but carefully avoiding building an empire on the British model, which would have to be managed and maintained. The US Navy, which was insignificant in 1880, was second only to the Royal Navy by 1907.

In the latter part of the nineteenth century America and Europe continued to look for new markets for their industrial production and all eyes were turned to the Far East. India was beginning to develop its industry, and Indian tea and cotton were penetrating markets which had been largely controlled by Britain and America. People as well as goods were on the move, with a significant exodus of Chinese people going to Australia and America, while people from a number of European countries were looking for opportunities in the New World. Even the methods of transport were undergoing major changes with the transition from sail to steam, and the building of railways in countries which had previously not had the facility for large numbers of people to travel quickly across great distances. The opening of the Suez Canal in 1869 was another step forward, which cut three thousand miles off the journey from England to China, and by dramatically reducing travel times brought people and markets closer together. The move from sail to steam also had a significant side effect, in that steamships required much more substantial quays and docks than wooden sailing ships, and there was a huge demand for hard Cornish granite which was an ideal building material for docks and harbours across the world. Another side effect of all these changes was the movement of missionaries, who followed in the steps of the traders, and not only brought their explicit version of the gospel to other nations, but also an implicit example of western life and values.

Joseph, who was the eldest Lewis child, was born in 1856 in Stabæk, which suggests that Arthur and Ellen had settled in Norway sometime in the early 1850s and were well-enough integrated into the country to have their own smallholding and to have become part of the local community. The nineteenth century was a turbulent time for the countries which we now call Scandinavia, and although Norway was historically a country in its own right, it had been under Danish rule for over four centuries, and probably would have remained so for some time to come if it had not been for Denmark's unwise involvement in the Napoleonic Wars, ending up on the side of the defeated. In the early years of the conflict the people of Norway had suffered severely from the blockading of Norwegian ports by the English and Russian fleets, which had led to dire conditions and widespread starvation, particularly in rural areas.

In 1814, under the Treaty of Kiel, Denmark was forced to cede Norway to Sweden, but this reverse had the effect of awakening Norwegians from a centuries-long sleep, and with a rising pride in nationhood, Norway took this opportunity to declare independence, and adopted a constitution based on the American and French models. In the same year, Christian Frederick was made King of Norway, on 17th May, which has since then been celebrated as Norwegian Constitution Day, the famous Syttende Mai. Not surprisingly, Sweden did not take kindly to Norway's aspirations and a desultory Norwegian-Swedish War ensued, but neither side was militarily strong enough to gain an advantage. By November 1814 a settlement had been negotiated in which Norway and Sweden were united as a dual monarchy, and Norway was able to retain its liberal constitution and to control its institutions, although Denmark took precedence in the control of foreign policy.

All this took place well before Arthur Lewis came to Norway, but these events set in train movements in Norwegian society that determined the structure and pattern of life for the whole country, and set the scene for the present day. Following union with Sweden, there was a rise in a kind of national romanticism encouraged by the works of Rousseau, which brought the previously ignored peasant farmer to a position centre stage in which he was portrayed as the salt of the earth, and the concept has been preserved in a community structure which is fundamentally based on farms and hamlets even today. The record of Arthur and his family in the census returns of the time document his farmstead, including his cattle numbers and area for potatoes, but it identifies his whereabouts by the farm cluster to which he belonged rather than by the name of a village or town.

At a national level, the area of the country which was capable of cultivation was naturally limited, with the result that a very considerable increase in population during the century caused problems, because without land people could not set up new homesteads and consequently began to look elsewhere to settle. A tide of emigration developed which was initially focussed on America where the Homestead Law of 1862, which granted land to immigrants, turned a trickle into a steady flow. People were greatly influenced by the stories which came back in letters and newspaper articles from emigrants, which extolled the freedom and opportunities of North America. It was an exact parallel to the same kind of reports which filtered back, during the same period, to people in Cornwall, from the hard-rock miners who had gone to the Americas and Australia to look for work and to escape food shortages and unemployment at home.

Apart from being driven by the need to find land to cultivate, many Norwegian emigrants were also motivated by a desire to find a freer form of society which was less dominated by the Lutheran Church. Compulsory confirmation had been introduced with stringent literacy requirements for reading the scriptures, which had the interesting side effect of stimulating the development of the education system. Despite the benefits created for schooling, many people found the ecclesiastical influence on their lives too intrusive, and the tenor of its effect can be felt even in the census returns that had a column for the date of baptism coming before the date of birth. Arthur and his children all scored a resounding double zero in the baptism column, and the final column for 'remarks' made it clear that the family belonged to a dissenting Baptist church that was only recognized by the state in 1845, and then only because it was part of an Act of Parliament that required births, deaths and marriages to be notified to the local Lutheran pastor.

Arthur settled the family on a farm which was part of a cluster which was collectively called Stabæk, in the municipality of Bærum in the county of Akershus, and it was there that the first five children were born. Bærum is located on the coast and now forms an affluent suburb on the western side of Oslo, although earlier in its history it was an industrial site with extensive lime kilns, and even before William the Conqueror came to England, Bærum was exporting quicklime for mortar through Slependen and Sandvika. In the seventeenth century iron ore was discovered, and the ironworks of Bærum Verk was started, soon to be followed by paper mills, a nail factory, sawmills, glassworks and brickworks. Alongside this development of industry there was a thriving agriculture on the productive soil beside the rivers Lysakerelven and Sandvikselva, and the remnants of extensive orchards can still be seen there today. Bærum is dominated by its craggy coastline running beside the Oslofjord, with hilly areas rising to the north and east with large areas of forest and numerous lakes. Today, the more rural area is protected from the intrusion of too many cars and is a perfect place for camping and fishing, while the original Stabæk has been built over and is now described as 'a transportation hub'. The Stabæk which Fritz and his family knew, was bordered on one side by forests and lakes, and on the other side by the sea, which left an indelible mark on all the members of the family, and particularly on Fritz and two of his elder brothers, who would spend much of their working lives on ships. Even though Fritz came back to England when he was only five, he was part of a family that spent a lot of its time, especially in summer, out of doors, and it was in Norway that he learned to swim and become familiar with boats. Bærum also had a more subtle influence because of the combination of light and colour, which attracted a number of artists to the area in much the same way that parts of Cornwall became artists' settlements. The names of the Norwegian painters are less familiar to English ears than their French counterparts, particularly the French Impressionists, but artists such as Fritz Thaulow, Christian Skredsvig, Kitty Kielland and the Lysaker Circle, with Eilif Pettersen, Gerhardt Munthe and Erik Werenskiold were among those who had studied in Christiania and who came back to Bærum in later life to live. The Lysaker Circle, in particular, had settled there and was instrumental in bringing about a turning point in Norwegian art through the 1880s. Although these painters and illustrators are more usually compared with their counterparts in Europe, they were developing their ideas at very much the same time as the Newlyn artists in Cornwall were attracted by the same sense of the open air and the special effects of light on the sea. Fritz would have been only dimly aware of the Bærum artists, but when he lived in Cornwall he came to know the marine artists Charles Napier Hemy and Henry Scott Tuke, as well as Winnie Freeman, one of his wife's aunts, all of whom found inspiration in the colours and light effects of Cornwall. Something of this experience in Norway found its way into Fritz's blood and made him always want to be near to the sea, and preferably on it or in it.

In 1939, before war made travel impossible, Fritz brought his wife May to Norway to see where he and his family had lived, and to spend some time in Oslo itself. Strangely, the guidebooks of today like to focus on a relatively recent emancipation of Oslo as the 'Nordic City of Light', and describe Christiania of the 1880s and 1890s as a dour place, depicted by Edvard Munch in paintings of men and women dressed all in black, with chalk-white faces, whom he described as 'the living dead who wend their tortuous way down the road that leads to the grave'. Happily there were other people who recorded their impressions of that time and who gave a rather different picture. Despite anguished warnings about the dangers, Lady Di Beauclerk was taken to Norway by her mother in 1868 as a change from 'visits to country houses and trips to Scotland',[3] and they were so enchanted that they decided to remain in Christiania for the winter. They watched as the fjord froze over and they heeded the local advice not to wear veils in the very cold weather in case their breath should freeze on them and might then freeze their noses, which they were warned, would become as brittle as china and could be broken off by an accidental blow. Lady Di described the delights of the Skating Club which created areas specially cleared of snow and flooded with water to freeze into a rink and 'was to Christiania what Rotten Row is to London. It has fashionable hours 12-2, unfashionable 2-4 and townsfolk by moonlight or torch'.[4] The Beauclerk ladies spent a contented winter in the city with its theatres, museums and public galleries and were never tempted, even at its coldest moments, to describe it as grey or dour, so perhaps Edvard Munch should not have the last word. Fritz and May were delighted by their stay in Oslo, even as the dark clouds of war were gathering very close by and which might well have cast a gloom over the city.

The Norwegian settlement pattern differed from England in that its parishes were subdivided into individual farms rather than

---

[3] Beauclerk, *Summer and Winter in Norway*, p.1.

[4] Ibid., p.113.

villages. Houses might cluster round a farm and form a small community, but the place carried the name of the farm, which was also often added to the family surname and changed if the family moved to another farm. The Lewis family retained its English pattern of naming and seemed to find its own place in the local community, and employed Norwegian servants, one of whom was to accompany the family to England when the time finally came to leave. Meanwhile life continued at Stabæk, and the family grew in size with the birth of another girl in 1864. Everything began well with little Ellen's arrival on 23rd March, but it was not long before her mother was pregnant again and a miscarriage followed in August, which would have been bad enough, if it had not been followed by her toddler's deteriorating health which ended in her death the following year. It was a devastating blow, and it took a long time for her mother to recover. Stabæk, which had been the scene of so much happiness, became a place marked by sorrow, and Ellen was unable to settle back into the old pattern of life without being continually reminded of what she had lost. Not for the last time, Arthur decided that there was nothing for it but to move to somewhere new, so the family left Stabæk and moved a short distance to a new holding at Holte, in East Bærum, where it was at last possible to try and put the events of the fateful year behind them. It seemed to work, because Charles was born in 1865 and the old two-year pattern of births was restored with the arrival of Walter followed by Norah, Fritz and Ralph.

Ellen was fifteen years younger than her husband Arthur, and although she had been twenty-four when Joseph was born, she was forty-three by the time that the last child, Ralph, arrived. Constant childbearing had taken its toll on what had been not the most robust of constitutions, although the only surviving photograph of Ellen shows a determined woman, who would not have shrunk from the task of bearing and bringing up a family of seven boys and two girls, on a smallholding that made its own demands on time and energy. The effort demanded over twenty years had however been too much. Ellen was not well and she wanted to be back in England where she felt that she really belonged. Arthur was by this time over sixty, and he too was feeling that it was time to return to the land of his birth, so everything was put on board ship, and the family sailed out of Oslo heading for a new life in Cornwall.

The arrival of Fritz and his family in Falmouth in 1877/78, brought about by his mother's deteriorating health, was not the happiest of events. The Norwegian air had served its purpose for twenty years and had enabled Ellen, not only to produce a family of seven lively boys and two girls, but also to establish a secure home where her children were able to go to school and grow up in a small and familiar community. Arthur had become an established figure in Bærum and local people found him an understanding and empathetic doctor, so it took something as serious as Ellen's illness to make him uproot his family and set sail from Christiania for a new but unknown life in Cornwall. Stepping off the boat in Falmouth were Arthur and Ellen with five of their sons, two daughters and their Norwegian servant Fianna Hansen, who was by then in her late thirties.

The family squeezed into their new home at 22 Harbour Terrace and immediately felt the impact of close terrace housing, separated from neighbours, with all their unfamiliar noises, by a solid but not soundproof party wall. The open spaces of Norway had disappeared, and there were no patients coming to tether their horses outside the house and wait to see Dr Lewis. As Ellen became less and less well, an air of foreboding settled over the house, and the carefree life of Scandinavia seemed a long way off.

On 1st June 1879 the end came and Ellen died at home of an abdominal tumour and what the doctor described as Mihal Disease. She had been carefully nursed by Fianna Hansen who was with her when she died and who then went to register her death. Arthur had begun to make his mark in Falmouth, but the *Falmouth Packet* simply referred to Ellen, as 'the wife of Arthur Lewis MRCS, who died aged 47'. There is no mention of her first name, and although it is probably symptomatic of the time, it makes her death seem more remote and impersonal than it was. Perhaps the newspapers were, in any case, more focussed on events elsewhere, as the same edition of the paper featured the story of the 17th Lancers and Royal Artillery embarking at Portsmouth to go to the Zulu War.

Fritz was seven when his mother died and his younger brother Ralph was just five. For the second time in his life Arthur knew that he needed to move the family to somewhere new, with more space and with readier access to the sea. After a brief search, he decided on a house overlooking the bay, which he felt was the right place to provide what was wanted, without being too far from the shops and the part of the town which had become familiar. As soon as possible after Ellen's death, the family moved to 8 Melvill Road, with views out to sea from the upstairs windows. The rooms were bigger and lighter than Harbour Terrace and there was more space at the back and a small garden at the front. Although the house at Harbour Terrace always afforded ready views of the constant activity of the harbour, Melvill Road was only a few minutes from the sea front, and it offered new horizons to a family that needed to find a fresh focus in its life. The task now was to settle into a new home, put down roots, and discover what the future might hold. The great advantage of doing this in Falmouth was that it was, and is, a place with some in-built characteristics which make it ideal for the starting and ending of stories. Over the years, a typical image of Falmouth has been captured in pictures of yachtsmen and women beginning and finishing great expeditions by passing between Black Rock and the St Anthony lighthouse at the entrance to the harbour. Falmouth is a place from where people have set out on new adventures, returning some time later to savour what they have achieved and to be welcomed by a community that understands such things, and will turn out on Castle Point, and wait at the Customs House Quay, to say 'welcome home'. Falmouth is not however a place which has happened by accident, and as Fritz came to know it better he began to understand something of what made it such a special place for him, in which he would be formed as a young man, and to where he would return from adventure and settle down to live and bring up his own family. Geography has played its part in the significance of Falmouth, but it has been particular individuals and families which have given the town its own distinctive character, and to understand the context in which Fritz grew up, there is a need to step back for a moment and look at Victorian Falmouth and the people who helped to develop it.

PART TWO

CORNWALL

Chapter 2

FOXES, COXES and FREEMANS

Fritz was five when his mother's deteriorating health meant that she needed to be brought back to England and his father had to decide where to settle the family. Arthur's roots had been in the Midlands and it might have been logical to pick up old links and go back to familiar ground, but the original move to Norway had been to find sea air for Ellen's lungs and so the coast was a must, but why so far south-west ? It may be that Arthur had come into contact with the Fox family in their consular role and that this had made a connection with the town, but whatever it was, Falmouth seemed to him to have exactly what was needed. The extremely cold winters of Norway were replaced by the wonderfully mild climate of Cornwall, and Falmouth itself had the sounds and smell of the sea, coupled with something of the light and landscape which had been such an attractive part of life in Bærum. There was a similarity too in the uncertain atmosphere of change which had been readily apparent in Norway and was also present in Cornwall, caused in both countries by the loss of their younger men and women in large-scale emigration to the new opportunities overseas. There was also a more subtle parallel in that both Norway and Cornwall were places where imagination and innovation were fostered by necessity, although this was not acknowledged by outsiders, and was not readily recognized even by insiders. As Cornish people suffered a serious sense of decline and looked overseas for new possibilities, they were in danger of forgetting the history and strength of their own heritage. Copper and tin had been produced in Cornwall from Bronze Age times, and the resulting trade with other countries meant that the Cornish had an awareness of other nations, well beyond their own boundaries. There had always been a sense in which people had looked outwards from Cornwall across the oceans, and Cornish engineering had been in demand from distant places, and yet the importance and achievements of Cornwall have rarely been acknowledged in the rest of Britain.

In the final quarter of the nineteenth century, when the Lewis family came to Harbour Terrace, Falmouth had grown in population from 9,500 in the early 1870s and would be just over 11,000 by the end of the century. It was a small enough place for people to become familiar with local characters, as illustrated in Caroline Fox's journals that show how people were aware of each other's presence and place in society, and how that was sometimes enshrined in local history. The two tall chimneys on Pennance Point, built to draw the arsenic-laden fumes out of the mine workings at Swanpool, were known locally as 'Anna Maria' and 'Caroline' in reference to the famous Fox sisters. The chimneys, which were familiar landmarks to Fritz, were tall and straight, like the sisters in their narrow Quaker dresses, in contrast to the billowing crinolines worn by other Victorian women of the time. The chimneys appeared to be walking down to the end of the point, just as the sisters would have walked there, leading a group of friends or visitors.

Members of the Fox family were readily recognized as they walked or drove around Falmouth, but there were other less well-known families who also played a significant part in the development of the town and a number of these people lived or worked within an area less than half a mile from Fritz's home in Melvill Road and would figure in his diaries. In the town opposite the Customs House were the business premises of the Cox brothers' chandlers and of Fox's shipping company. Not far away along Bar Road lived a number of shipwrights including Eddy Thomas at number 3a, whose family included Harold, one of Fritz's brothers, who had married Eddy's daughter Ada. Moored just off Thomas's boatyard was Henry Scott Tuke's barque, the *Julie of Nantes*, which doubled as a floating studio for the painter, and on which boy apprentices from Cox's engineering works earned pocket money as artist's models. Close by in the harbour was the *Vander-Meer*,[1] the floating studio of another marine artist, Charles Napier Hemy, who liked to paint sailing boats in action and drove some of his models to distraction by making them sail endlessly back and forth in front of him. At the top of the hill, above Bank House belonging to the Fox's, was Woodlane House, the home of John Freeman, the force behind the Freeman Granite business and the grandfather of May Page who would become Fritz's wife.

In order to understand the Falmouth in which Fritz grew up, there is a need to step back for a moment from the narrative of his life and delve behind the caricature which presents Cornwall as a place where there was mining activity in the early nineteenth century, which was neatly replaced by tourism. The story that is emerging with the help of those who have been putting new life into Cornish studies,[2] is that Cornwall became industrialized at a very early stage, and then exported its expertise and specialist equipment across the globe. From the end of the eighteenth century into the first half of the nineteenth century, Cornwall was the world leader in copper production as well as tin. Cornish beam engines for crushing the ore and pumping water out of mine workings were in demand across the world, as were the skills of Cornish hard-rock miners, as new discoveries of metal-bearing ores were made in South America, Canada, Australia and South Africa. As the focus for copper production moved elsewhere, Cornwall went through a very difficult period. The potato famine of the 1840s, which hit Cornwall with the same kind of devastation for the poor as in Ireland and Scotland, was followed by a fall in the copper market in the 1860s,

---

[1] Built in 1888, 57 feet overall, and based on the hull and lead keel of a yacht owned by Hemy.

[2] The Institute of Cornish Studies. Director, Philip Payton. See Bibliography.

and the decline for tin in the 1870s. The truth is, that although Cornwall had been one of the first places in the British Isles to become industrialized, it had become so specialized in mining that it had failed to diversify and broaden its industrial base and develop a wider range of supporting industries. Consequently, when mining went into decline, the whole economy followed, and Cornwall witnessed starvation in its mining communities and food riots in its towns. This part of Cornwall's history has often not received the attention it deserves, and the result has been that the life of the county in the second half of the nineteenth century has remained hidden. Just as Fritz was to enter China in a particular window in time, so he arrived in Cornwall as it reeled from its thriving industrial past, and tried to discern in what way it could move forward into a viable future. As he witnessed what was happening he came to know a number of families who played significant roles in the way that Cornwall developed, and who worked hard at trying to establish new industries and a new foundation for the Cornish economy. Three families in particular, the Foxes, the Coxes and the Freemans would figure in Fritz's diaries, and their innovative and entrepreneurial stories help to paint the picture of how Falmouth came to be the place that it was when Fritz arrived. The Foxes were involved in shipping and mining and it was their Perran Foundry, among others in West Cornwall, which manufactured state-of-the-art engines and machinery which served worldwide. The Freemans were strategic developers of the Cornish granite industry, at a time when iron steamships required solid stone docks and quays instead of wooden wharves. The Cox family is less well documented than the other two, but in addition to their involvement in local business and politics, they were the people who provided the shipbuilding and repairing facility that became the backbone of the Falmouth Docks, as well as being the driving force behind the setting up of the Falmouth and Penryn Waterworks Company, which would in due course become so much a part of Fritz's life.

THE FOXES

As the sixteenth and seventeenth centuries had witnessed the rise of the Killigrews in Cornwall, so the eighteenth century saw the rise in importance of the Fox family. By the middle of the century, George Croker Fox was well established at Fowey as a mine owner, merchant and shipping agent, having established the firm of G C Fox and Son. In 1799 Fox purchased the lease on Portreath Harbour on the north coast, and carried out an extensive reconstruction of the port to facilitate the export of copper ore to South Wales for smelting, and the importation of coal and timber for the mines. In 1809, Fox and Williams started to build the Portreath–Poldice tramway to link the port with the Gwennap mine, and together with various branch lines which they constructed, the company was able to exercise an almost total monopoly on traffic to and from the port. The digging of the mines and the construction of the tramways and railways has marked the landscape in this part of Cornwall to this day, although now the railways have been turned into scenic walks and cycle paths, which give the visitor something of an insight into what industrialized Cornwall was like, as they thread their way through a hugely pitted landscape. The open rough grazing and moorland which characterizes central inland Cornwall today, was at this time a mass of smoking mine workings with all the paraphernalia that was part and parcel of the process of extraction and transport of mineral ores. In its turn, this massive manual activity triggered a ferment of innovative thinking and invention in which Cornish men and women played a part, but for which they are not readily credited. Robert Fox, who played such a key role in the development of this part of Cornwall, and his wife Elizabeth (Tregelles) produced a large family of which two of their sons and two of their grandchildren left a particular mark on Falmouth. Their eldest son, confusingly given the same name as his father, became a nationally respected geologist and physicist who conducted an investigation into the reasons for high temperatures in Cornish mines. The accepted wisdom was that the heat came from the activities below ground, whereas Robert Fox began to explore the question of heat coming from the earth's core. It was this kind of research which helped to increase understanding of mining deep underground and resulted in Robert being made a Fellow of the Royal Society in 1848.

One of Robert's brothers, and the seventh son of Robert Fox senior and Elizabeth, was the scientific writer Charles Fox, who was also active in the family businesses, becoming a partner in G C & R W Fox & Co, the merchants and shipping agents in Falmouth. Charles was a founder member of the Royal Cornwall Polytechnic Society which was the brainchild of his nieces Caroline Fox the diarist, and her sister Anna Maria. The Polytechnic encouraged fresh thinking and invention, and among other initiatives it offered a premium of £300 for the design and construction of a 'man engine' which would assist miners in being lifted out of mines at the end of their shifts, instead of the huge effort involved in climbing endless ladders up narrow shafts. The first engine was erected at Tresavean mine at Gwennap in 1842, and proved a great success.

The unique role of the Polytechnic was that it enabled ordinary people to hear about new inventions that would otherwise be beyond their experience. Edison's phonograph was demonstrated by the 'eminent electrician' Professor Lynd, and the *Falmouth Packet* reported that 'few people can yet quite realise that the singing of Patti[3] and the voice of Her Majesty the Queen are as distinct and audible as if we were in their presence'.[4] Fritz was able to take advantage of hearing Polytechnic lectures and it was at one of these that he learned details of the invention of the domestic wireless.

Robert and Charles Fox were men who had a direct involvement in Cornish industry and who brought to it a specialist expertise and a Quaker concern for humanity, although it has to be said that women and children worked in their mines in appalling conditions. The incentive to innovate and push things forward remained with the Fox descendants, and it was largely through pressure from G C Fox & Co, that in 1872, the Post Office laid an overland cable from Falmouth to the Lizard, where the Foxes joined with William Broad & Co. to build a signal station at Bass Point, so that passing ships could signal the shore and the messages could then be passed on to agents in Falmouth.

---

[3] Adelina Patti, world famous lyric coloratura soprano.
[4] *Falmouth Packet*, 21st September 1889.

The influence of the Fox family also reached way beyond Cornwall, with international links which had an impact on the lives of people back home and affected the way in which people like Fritz regarded work and travel overseas. The great emigration from Cornwall, which began early in the nineteenth century and gathered pace as conditions became more difficult in the 1840s with the collapse of the world price for copper, was fuelled by developments abroad with which the Foxes were closely involved. The mining of newly discovered copper in Chile and Peru was hugely assisted by the emigration of Cornish miners and state-of-the-art Cornish mining equipment, and among the directors of the Chilean Mining Association were George C Fox and Alfred Fox, as well as the mining magnate members of the Williams family of Truro and Scorrier. Cornish engines and mechanical knowledge were in demand, and as early as 1811, enquiries about engines that would work at high level were reaching Cornwall. Francisco Uville from Switzerland came to England to seek advice from Boulton and Watt, only to find that their low-pressure pumping engine would not work efficiently at the high altitude of the Peruvian mines, some of which were 14,000 feet above sea level. Uville was however able to obtain a working model of a high-pressure steam engine, designed by the Cornish mine engineer and inventor Richard Trevithick, which worked perfectly at high level. The experiments were so successful that Richard Trevithick travelled to Peru in 1816 to see how his engines were working, and to sort out some of the problems which had developed. Trevithick worked in South America for some years, eventually travelling back to England via Costa Rica and Colombia, arriving in Falmouth in 1827. It is a strange twist of fate that the mining skills and engineering expertise of Cornwall were key factors in the rapid development of mining overseas, which had the cumulative effect of displacing Cornwall as the world leader in copper production.[5] It also seems unjust that Richard Trevithick, who played such an important part in the invention and development of steam locomotion should receive so little recognition outside Cornwall.

[5] Philip Payton, *The Cornish Overseas*, Ch. 3, for a fuller account.

By the beginning of the twentieth century and the time when Fritz was settling back into Falmouth after his travels, the Foxes had established themselves in a patriarchal role, and were therefore tending to be patrons and figureheads rather than being closer to the shop floor of industry as they had been in the eighteenth and nineteenth centuries. This did not detract from their continuing significance as people to whom appeal could be made when the docks needed to develop, or a telegraph cable needed to be laid, or the postmaster was short-staffed. It was a 'Mr Fox' along with Mr John Freeman who joined with other influential men of the day to bring pressure to bear to build a house in Church Street to accommodate the Postmaster, Newberry Cox.[6] The Foxes were at the top of a social pyramid and the entrepreneurial layers below needed them as a reference point, and the high regard in which the Foxes were held carried on into the next century and beyond. In Fritz's diaries there is a note of respect when he refers to any members of the Fox family, and his son Wilf always spoke in a slightly hushed tone about the Foxes of Woodlane and Penjerrick.

The Fox family was also an example of the way in which religion played a role in the development of Falmouth, partly because of the ties between different people of the same faiths which was expressed in business partnerships, and partly because of what churches and their members gave to the town for better or worse. The Foxes came from the strong Quaker tradition founded by George Fox who visited Cornwall in 1655, and whose influence steadily grew in the county after initial suspicion and persecution. John Wesley visited Cornwall in the mid 1700s and left perhaps an even more profound influence which was the root of Cornish Methodism, and as miners and others dispersed through emigration to the four corners of the earth they took with them their traditions and their religion. It was the Methodist respect for humanity that was so sharply challenged when Cornish emigrants came across the way that slaves and indigenous people were so often treated abroad. Stories of the ill-treatment of slaves in the Americas, and the Maoris and Aborigine people in New Zealand and Australia, filtered back

---

[6] S E Gay, *Old Falmouth.*

to Cornwall in letters, and from early in the century some returning emigrants made it their business to make sure that people at home knew what was happening abroad. When William Whitburn returned home to Gwennap in the autumn of 1839, he was asked to address the Redruth Institution on the subject of the Cobre Mine in Cuba, and he had some disparaging remarks to make about the Cuban people but reserved his strongest condemnation for the practice of slavery which existed in Cuba 'in its worst form'.[7] Stories brought back from round the world by returning Cornishmen helped to strengthen the growing revulsion of the slave trade, and Cornish people were early protagonists in the campaign to abolish slavery, although as usual, Cornwall's role has seldom been acknowledged from outside the county.

THE FREEMANS

The story of the Freemans in Cornwall is to a large extent the story of Cornish granite in its heyday. In the early nineteenth century a small number of local men had established a modest trade with London to supply granite for kerbs, but then came the plan for building Waterloo Bridge in granite that was an altogether much larger project with much greater demands. It happened that the Chairman of the Bridge Committee was Henry Swann, one of Penryn's two MPs, who is said to have formed a company to obtain granite from Mabe and Stithians for the bridge, although there is strangely no surviving record that this happened. However, the involvement of Penryn granite merchants did stimulate interest, and in London the Cornishmen were soon seen as a force to be taken seriously, and one that rapidly became more influential than their rivals in Aberdeen.

In the 1830s and 40s there were a number of local Penryn merchants who are recorded in *South West Granite*,[8] a study by Peter Stanier, but the whole tenor of the business went up several notches with the arrival in Cornwall of the Freemans, who had established a thriving business in Yorkshire under Joseph Freeman and had

[7] *West Briton*, 29th November 1839.
[8] *South West Granite*, 1999.

moved into the London scene supplying York paving stone. Joseph however died in 1808 and the business was then run by his redoubtable widow Sarah who was an extremely astute business woman in a tough male-dominated world in which she seems to have given no quarter. She was criticized in 1825 for trying to raise the price of York stone artificially by a mixture of pressurizing quarrymen in Yorkshire and holding back stone from the market by hoarding, although neither accusation was proved. Sarah had an unusually hard upbringing, being a descendant of a Huguenot family that had fled persecution in France and had come to England where she was born in 1771 and subsequently married Joseph Freeman in 1792 and bore ten children - two girls and eight boys. Although infant deaths were all too common at the time, Sarah seems to have had more than her share of tragedy. Of her eight boys only three reached the age of twenty, and four died under the age of four. One of the girls died as a baby and the death of the second is not recorded in the Freeman records but it was at an early age. Sarah's relationship with her three surviving sons was understandably very close, and they were protective of her as a young widow, but she was particularly fond of John who was nine at the time of his father's death.

In due course Sarah brought her sons into the business, and in 1829 William and John Freeman were listed as stone and marble merchants at 27 Millbank Street, Westminster where Sarah continued to live and provide a London base for her family. Today it seems an odd place from which to manage a stone merchants but at the time it was right beside the company's wharves on the banks of the Thames, on the piece of land which is now the Victoria Tower Gardens between the Houses of Parliament and Lambeth Bridge. In 1888 the Freemans occupied a vacant site beside the Brewer's Arms public house at the Lambeth Bridge end of Millbank Street (numbers 55 and 57) until 1907 when the whole area was redeveloped and made into the park that we see today. Around 1841 William became blind and stayed in London for the day-to-day running of the business from Millbank Street, while John settled his family in Plymouth where the company had premises, and travelled the country picking up contracts and gaining first-hand knowledge of quarries throughout the British Isles. It was not long before John realized the potential of granite in Cornwall and he was quick to recognize the strategic importance of Penryn, which he made his centre of operations in the county, building Freeman's yard there with its convenient quay for loading ships. As Cornwall steadily became the focus of the Freeman Granite operation, it was logical for John to move his family from Plymouth to Falmouth, and a letter from the George Street Baptist Church in Plymouth was sent to the Baptist Church in Falmouth commending 'our Christian friends Mr and Mrs (John) Freeman and their six daughters, to your care and oversight'.[9] The family was welcomed with open arms by the Reverend S H Booth of Falmouth and almost at once John Freeman was elected as a deacon, and within a short time his son John Deane Freeman and his wife were also transferred from Plymouth to Falmouth. John Freeman senior was well respected by his workforce and he was remembered for building chapels near his quarry workings in recognition of the dangers of the work, and the need for men to have a place to rest and worship. On a practical front he was also responsible for founding the British Workman's Institute in Falmouth, while his son John Freeman junior helped to found the Falmouth YMCA.

At the outset the business did not require huge investment because the Freemans could contract gangers to obtain suitable blocks of stone from a large number of quarries willing to supply them. Even so, the size of the contracts negotiated by the Freemans meant that the company needed to be able to tap an ever larger number of potential suppliers, since from the 1840s onwards, granite was being sent for major dock works at Plymouth, Chatham, Hull and Liverpool. The development of iron steamships had precipitated the need for much more substantial port and dock facilities, and this was happening all over the world, with Freeman Granite being used for building docks in Bombay, Buenos Aires, Malta and Gibraltar. The Freemans had entered the right business at the right time as granite became the must-have material for the

---

[9] L A Fereday, *The Story of Falmouth Baptists*

The balcony course for the Fastnet Lighthouse dry-set for inspection at Freeman's Yard in Penryn before being shipped to Rock Island for construction.

job, and the company had the foresight to recognize that there needed to be a middleman between quarry and end-user, and this was an expertise that they were able to exercise to the full. The Penryn yard was the place where the rough blocks were cut and finished ready for being transported to wherever they were required. Photographs in a company publicity booklet[10] show the finished stones for the balcony course of the Fastnet Lighthouse being dry-set at Penryn for inspection, before being shipped out. The Freemans understood the need for precision in stone cutting and finishing, as well as managing the logistics of shifting very large dead weights, and they were careful to capitalize on the new railways for providing transport. There are many illustrations of the day-to-day task of moving enormous granite blocks using horses or steam power, and the noise and drama is well illustrated in an account written by an observer at the time.

Mention should be made of Freeman's famous traction engine to haul the granite from quarries to yard; iron-rimmed wheels,

[10] *CORNISH GRANITE: Its History, Legends and Modern Uses.* Undated.

Conveying the Die Stone of the King Alfred Memorial, Winchester, from the quarry to the railway. The rear traction engine was used to assist in steering on the narrow Cornish roads.

no rubber tyres in those days, engines weighing about 13 or 14 tons, pulling unsprung wagons (three at a time) each weighing about 3 or 3 ½ tones, and carrying three loads of 8 to 10 or 12 tons according to size of blocks. When one of these loads was coming downhill to Penryn, the screeching of the brakes could be heard all over the town, and up past the railway station. Some of these Fowler engines were named *Alpha, Beta, Epsilon and Zeta*. There was also one Burrell-type engine [called *Her Majesty*] weighing over 14 tons. Once about 1920 or 1921 the brakes failed and the whole lot ran away, crashing near the railway bridge and breaking the main axle of the engine. The main road was blocked for several days whilst emergency repairs were carried out.[11]

By 1866 John Freeman had brought his sons John Deane and William George into the firm, which was now called John Freeman & Sons, and all three were living in Falmouth. The sons had become well established in Cornwall and had taken over the running of the

---

[11] From personal notes made by Mr Abraham, who worked for the Freeman company 1912-1948.

business by the time their father died at his home at Woodlane House in 1874.

As Fritz grew up he became steadily more aware of the influence of the Freemans on Cornwall, and especially on the town where they lived. John's widow, Mary Deane, continued to live on Woodlane after Woodlane House itself had been demolished, and Fritz knew Mary as an old lady living at 18 Woodlane with three of her unmarried daughters, including Alice and Sophie who had an especially soft spot for the young Fritz because of the budding romance between him and their niece May.

THE COXES

The Fox and Freeman families have been well documented by historians, and the Foxes in particular have the benefit of the published journals of Caroline and Barclay Fox that give vivid glimpses of Cornwall in the late nineteenth and early twentieth centuries. The Cox family, on the other hand, receives passing mentions by writers, but usually only as brief acknowledgements. Most descriptions of the development of the Falmouth Docks refer to the two brothers, Joseph Goodenough Cox and Henry Herbert Cox, coming to Falmouth and forming a partnership as ships' chandlers, and then responding to demand by establishing a foundry

Joseph Goodenough Cox   Henry Herbert Cox

and smithy connected with the docks, but this is only a fraction of what the Cox family contributed to the town.

The docks company was set up following a first general meeting on 16th June 1859 with 230 shareholders and Mr Alfred Fox as Chairman. The company had acquired 180 acres of freehold land but had to fight the Duchy of Cornwall and the Ecclesiastical Commissioners for the right to make use of the foreshore, and the case was only finally settled in court by a payment of £1,500 to the plaintiffs. After that, matters moved quickly and the foundation stone was laid with all due ceremony orchestrated by the Freemasons on 28th February 1860. The name, the Falmouth Docks Company, described precisely what the role of the business was, in that it built and owned the docks but it was not a shiprepairing contractor, and it therefore needed to encourage local shipwrights to supply that particular service, for which the company rented space for repairers to set up their workshops. It was this opportunity which attracted the Cox brothers, who had already added an iron foundry and smithy to their chandlery business because they had spotted an important gap in the market, and with the docks right on their doorstep, they were perfectly placed to respond to the rapidly growing demand. In 1868 the Coxes moved their premises to the

Laying the Foundation Stone of the Falmouth Docks on 28th February 1860
(Illustrated London News)

west side of Western Wharf and changed the name of their business to the Docks Foundry and Engineering Company, which later became Cox, Farley and Company. Fritz served his apprenticeship with Cox's in the early 1890s and by 1909, when he was settled back in Falmouth as a married man, the business had become the limited company of Cox & Company (Engineering) Ltd. The involvement of the Coxes with Falmouth Docks is only one aspect of the achievements of what must have been one of the most extraordinary entrepreneurial families to come to Falmouth in the nineteenth century.

The Cox's story began in Somerset with James Blatch Cox, who was recorded in the 1841 census, as a Baptist minister at Hatch Beauchamp near Taunton. Presumably James had some additional income over and above what he earned as a minister, because the household included Mary Criddle as governess for his children, all of whom would play leading roles when the family moved to Cornwall. The eldest was James junior, who shared the schoolroom with his brother Newberry, who would in due course become the Falmouth postmaster. Joseph Goodenough and Henry Herbert who founded the chandlers and the engineering works, were duly added to the family and came under the care of the governess along with their sisters Harriott and Elizabeth who would become noted Falmouth ironmongers. It appears that James senior was part of a well-established Cox family in Somerset and one that was involved in foundry work near Taunton, and he was therefore well placed to bring up a thriving family which would leave its mark in Cornwall.

Life as a Baptist minister seems not to have been to James's liking, and he probably did not take kindly to feeling that he was at the beck and call of his local congregation and ultimately largely under their direction. The history of the Falmouth Baptists[12] in their early days demonstrates how quickly a minister could fall foul of a significant section of the congregation and could be simply asked to leave after a vote of church members. Whatever happened in Somerset, it was fairly dramatic because the census of 1851 shows

[12] L A Fereday, *The Story of Falmouth Baptists.*

James, at the age of fifty, installed in Dispensary Court on Market Street in Falmouth, as proprietor of an ironmongery business, and described in the Williams Commercial Directory as a 'china and earthenware dealer'. James had moved his family from Somerset in 1843, and as well as the ironmongers, he added an additional string to his bow as the Falmouth agent for the Norwich Union Life Assurance Company. An advertisement for annuities appeared regularly on the front page of the *Falmouth Packet*, although prospective clients may have been slightly mystified by the fact that the agent's office was in an ironmonger's shop.

James's sons, Joseph Goodenough and Henry Herbert, settled into their new life by the sea and were as quick as their father in seeing a business opportunity, and it was not long before they had joined forces to set up their chandlery. Meanwhile James continued to apply himself with considerable energy to his new career, so much so that within three years he was sufficiently established in the town to be elected Mayor of Falmouth for two years in 1846, and later served another term in 1854. If he had lived, he would have been proud to see his grandson Alfred Cox occupying the same post in 1907/08.

It might seem that James Cox senior had done as much as might be reasonably expected of a man of his age in such a short time, but that would be to underestimate the ability and drive of this extraordinary man. In the 1861 census, James had reached the age of sixty and the family was then living at College Wood, but the surprise is in James's occupation, because by that time he was listed as the Manager of the Falmouth and Penryn Waterworks, a post which he still occupied ten years later when he was seventy. In the mid nineteenth century there was a crying need throughout the country for towns to have a regular and properly managed supply of good quality water, and even with the insights provided by Charles Dickens in his novels, there seems to be little real grasp even today of how dire things were for the poor in early Victorian England, especially those living in overcrowded conditions in towns.

The initiative to set up a waterworks came from a group of private individuals who probably saw it more as a commercial opportunity than a service to the town, though they were ready enough to use the latter argument in their proposals which required an Act of Parliament to allow the company to extract water from rivers and springs, and construct a reservoir on high ground above Penryn. The proposers of the scheme comprised a partnership of local businessmen together with some influential financial backers based in London. Among the local men were Henry Herbert Cox and a 'Mr Harvey' of Penryn who farmed the land on which the reservoir was to be built, but as often happens in Cornwall, the real power was retained by the outside parties, comfortably distanced from any local connection. If there was tension between the Falmouth and the London directors of the company, it paled into insignificance compared to the fraught relationship which subsequently developed between the waterworks company and Falmouth Town Council, and which ultimately resulted in the employment of Fritz as a troubleshooter to sort out the practical difficulties. The root of the problem went right back to the beginning, when the company applied to parliament to extract water from the College River flowing through Penryn, and to store water in a new reservoir to be built in the catchment area below Mabe. In January 1847 the *Falmouth Packet* carried a notice to the effect that two commissioners were coming to Selley's Hotel later in the month 'for the purpose of making a local examination and survey of the district comprised in the proposed bill [to come before Parliament] for supplying Falmouth with water, and for hearing any opposition which may be made to the same'. The Commissioners,[13] J M Herbert and T Page, were left in no doubt by the evidence brought before them that the need for a proper water supply for the town was a matter of considerable urgency, as had been demonstrated in some detail by Dr W H Bullimore of Truro in two lectures that he had given in 1846 on 'The Health of Towns', in which he had raised serious questions about the lack of proper sewers and safe water

---

[13] Report of the Inquiry relating to the proposed Falmouth Waterworks Bill, 1847. Minutes of Evidence.

supply in any town, but particularly Falmouth. Others were equally concerned but less willing to appear in public, and had to content themselves with letters to the *Falmouth Packet*, like the one from 'An Inhabitant' published on 25th August 1846 which complained of 'the dung heap and pig sty [for fifteen pigs] which was only separated from the main street by a low wall.' The resulting smell and its effects on people living nearby were graphically described.

A primary concern was one of health, and typhoid raged in Falmouth in 1832 with 120 deaths, and there were further serious outbreaks in 1848 and 1849. There was a lack of any kind of sewer system apart from three short lengths, comprising only 230 yards in total, with outlets into the harbour at the foot of Market Strand, the Fish Strand and Bank. The evidence of the doctors in the town was particularly telling, and they described overflowing cesspits, filth left in piles to be collected by the night carts, and an all-pervading smell from which there was no relief, and the whole situation was made worse by the lack of water to wash down the streets or run through the sewers that did exist. However, it was not only the stink and sickness which were a problem, but the additional risks from fires that could not be put out because of the lack of water for hoses, and which could result in the loss of whole lines of houses when a fire broke out in one of the close-packed dwellings. A further complication came from the demands of up to 3,000 ships coming into the harbour each year and needing to take on fresh water, which was supposed to be available from a government-built reservoir sited near the church at Mylor, from which a floating tank, owned and managed by a Mr Husband, ferried water to the waiting ships. Even this arrangement had its problems because the floating tank was unable to operate in bad weather, and could in any case not load up at low tide. The result was that ships sent crew members into the town to try and get water from the public fountain or private wells with predictable aggravation, and often returned empty-handed, so that their vessels left the port without having taken sufficient water on board.

The dire need for a properly regulated water supply was obvious, and it was also clear that the existing arrangements were simply unable to cope in any way with demand. The Inquiry heard, that apart from private wells, there were five public pumps, three stand cocks, two wells and a fountain in the market place to provide the needs of a town of 10,000 people. The public pumps were unlocked from six to ten o'clock in the morning and then closed until four o'clock, when they were unlocked for three hours until being secured again at seven in the evening. It was not unusual to see anything from twenty to sixty people waiting in a queue for the pumps to be opened, and even then, some went away empty-handed when the water ran out, and had to try to beg water from private wells. Unbelievably, matters got worse in the summer months when the water supply often failed altogether, and supplies had to be brought in from Flushing at the rate of three gallons for a penny, and more than that if the water had to be brought round by horse and cart.

Against this background it is extraordinary that a small but significant body of people was opposed to any proposals for a waterworks, and expressed great anxiety about details of disease and insanitary living conditions being made public, and consequently damaging the reputation of the town. The evidence to the Inquiry was a clear demonstration of one half of a town having no idea whatever how the other half was living, and some witnesses were able to compare the extreme filth in the poor areas with what a churchwarden described as the 'extreme cleanliness of smaller rate-payer's houses'. The links between the two worlds were provided by doctors and churchmen, who were the only people to give evidence who had first-hand knowledge of how people lived on either side of the divide. At this stage the *Falmouth Packet* was strangely silent on the subject of the waterworks, and apart from carrying the advertisement of the public inquiry, confined its comments to a report of a town council meeting in which a group of councillors was appointed to act as observers at the Inquiry 'to prevent the parliamentary bill containing any proposals which might be injurious to the town'. There was scarcely another word written on the subject for the remainder of the year, in sharp contrast to the extensive column inches devoted to the new railways to be constructed in

Cornwall, which had recently been sanctioned by parliamentary acts, together with the weekly reports on the activities of the police, the rumours of rampant 'Puseyism' in the parish church, and the inadequacy of the town gas supply for public lighting, which had resulted in shops having to close early for lack of light. The *Packet* always included regular reports of town council meetings, so the lack of any news of the waterworks indicates that it was not a subject which was discussed in any more detail by councillors, at least in public, and it leaves a question as to whether the mayor was less than enthusiastic about having the subject on the agenda.

In the end the Commissioners were more than satisfied, and most of the objectors to the waterworks scheme withdrew their opposition when faced with the weight of evidence presented to the Inquiry. By an Act of Parliament of 1847 the Falmouth and Penryn Waterworks came into being and was permitted to build a reservoir of 179,200 cubic feet above Penryn, and to abstract and store water from the College River, and also draw water from springs in the watershed area. The waterworks itself was to be built in Penryn beside the river and water was to be piped in a nine-inch main to Market Strand in Falmouth, with a four-inch branch taken out past Greenbank, with another along Church Street and Arwenack Street and a third going up Killigrew Street. However, it was the structure of the Waterworks Company which was interesting, although it excited little comment in the Inquiry itself. The initiative for setting up the company came partly from Falmouth with at least two local directors, but the other three directors were all based in London, and as the saga continued it became clear that the Falmouth dog was being wagged by its London tail. Even more significant in terms of its later history, the Waterworks Company was apparently unable to excite enough interest for local people to invest in the company, and even Falmouth Town Council resisted being drawn into the enterprise. There was however a twist to the story in that James Blatch Cox was Mayor of Falmouth in 1847 and attended the Inquiry as an interested and helpful observer, and if the Commissioners had known that he was to be the first manager of the new waterworks, they might have been more suspicious of his helpful interventions in the proceedings, which with hindsight, were more concerned with promoting the rights and opportunities of the Waterworks Company than with the good of Falmouth Town Council. The interests of the Cox family were well served, but the lack of involvement of the local authority was something which would come back to haunt Falmouth, and the first signs of the problem emerged within five years, as it was realized that there needed to be some kind of properly constituted body to take responsibility for a sewerage system, which was not part of the remit of the waterworks. A widely supported petition was submitted to the General Board of Health for an inspection under the terms of the Public Health Act 1848, into the sewerage, drainage and supply of water for the Borough and Parish of Falmouth. In 1854, the Inspector, Robert Rawlinson Esq., came to Falmouth and heard evidence which highlighted the rate of deaths from 'zymotic deseases' and one witness spoke of some Falmouth living conditions being 'as bad as those I visited in London'.[14] Dr Bullimore said that 'some places and cases are so bad that I would rather give double the fee I am paid to anyone else to attend'.

One of the witnesses to give evidence was, not surprisingly, the Waterworks Manager James Blatch Cox, who said that the water supply was constant and at high pressure and supplied 490 customers with taps in their homes, and the rest of the town with 180 external taps for communal use. The company also undertook to lay a service pipe to any property in the town at a cost of ten shillings, provided that the distance did not exceed fifteen feet from the main. As far as the Waterworks Company was concerned there seemed to be no problem with either the supply of water or its quality, but the report of the Inquiry was less happy and commented that 'at present the water is dull and turbid' though it was recommended that this could be removed by filtration. It was also recommended that galvanised and iron pipes were better suited to the soft water of the area than lead piping which was often eaten away completely.

---

[14] Robert Rawlinson Esq., *Report to the General Board of Health*, 1854.

The Waterworks Company had only been in existence for seven years and the evidence that it gave to the Inquiry had more than a hint of being defensive of its record, so it was sensitive to public opinion and responded positively to a little horse-trading by the Inspector. The company had proposed a charge to house owners of ten shillings a year for water closets and the same for baths, but the Inspector managed to get an agreement to reduce the charge to five shillings and even managed to persuade the company to supply water free to public baths and wash houses, whereas it was going to charge five shillings. Other charges remained as proposed, including an annual charge of twelve shillings for houses with a horse and carriage, a pound for two horses at the same address and eight shillings for each additional horse. The Inquiry heard many of the same concerns that had been raised when the waterworks was first being set up. The quality of water was not good and there was a recommendation that filtering through sand should be part of the supply process with catch pits built below the reservoir. The other major concern was the interruption of the supply at frequent intervals, particularly in summer time, which was largely due to the company having to maintain water to three or four mills above Penryn, which had secured priority under the original Act of Parliament with rights of compensation. These issues, as well as a concern about the availability of water at fire hydrants to fight fires, continued to be a worry, and they resurfaced with some force towards the end of the century, with a series of reports that resulted in the company having to employ an inspector to sort out the problems. The first person to fill the inspector's post, and to serve for many years with the company, would be none other than Fritz Lewis.

A further example of the drive and commitment of the Cox clan can be glimpsed from a description of another of James Blatch Cox's sons, Newberry Cox, who became Falmouth Postmaster in 1856, at the tender age of twenty-three. Susan Gay,[15] whose own father worked for the Post Office, remembered Newberry Cox, and makes a tantalizing reference to Newberry's 'book of notes' in which

---

[15] S E Gay, *Old Falmouth.*

he recorded his daily experience in a job which brought him into close contact with virtually the whole local population. Newberry became Postmaster well after the old Packet establishment had been broken up and had been transferred to Plymouth, but foreign mails were still received and dispatched in Falmouth. This additional work was carried out by Newberry who was faithfully assisted by his wife, but without any other staff. Susan Gay records that 'sometimes he could hardly snatch a few moments for meals, and when the Plymouth mail was late, he would meet it half way to Truro, and receive the arriving mail from the coach, turn the guard back with the outward mail, and save the delivery to Falmouth. As he had to be on duty from seven in the morning, it goes without saying that he was not a little fagged out'.

The Postmaster's hours were from seven in the morning until ten at night, but Newberry was not a man to sleep if things needed to be done, and he recorded at one point in his notes that he had not had a full night's sleep for four years. The young Postmaster's problems were compounded by the frequent move of premises for the Post Office. He started in Post Office Yard before moving to Church Street and then a move across the street to the other side, followed by a spell on the Moor before going to Market Street and subsequently Bell's Court, where Newberry and his wife lived for six years. Part of the problem seems to have been that there was no allowance for expenses, and the responsibility for finding an office rested with the Postmaster, coupled with the need to have somewhere to live. The situation became sufficiently difficult for it to come to the attention of the men of substance in the town, and Newberry's efforts were 'seconded by Mr John Freeman, Messrs. Fox, Broad, and others [and] a house was built on the site of the two old cottages in Church Street, and this is where the present enlarged building stands [in 1903]'.[16] This was however not the end of Newberry's troubles, because he not only had problems with premises and housing but also with the continuing lack of staff. He had been in post for thirteen years before he finally managed to persuade the Post Office to provide a clerk who, of course, then had to be trained

[16] S E Gay, *Old Falmouth.*

up to Newberry's exacting standards, and also be willing to cope with long hours and heavy work. The mails from abroad were often considerable, and sometimes required a bus to transport them to Plymouth, and despite the end of the Packet service, some ship mails were still arriving in Falmouth as late as 1870. In typical style, Newberry was in the habit of saving time by sailing out to the steamers in his own boat in order to land the mail more quickly, and Susan Gay recorded that 'Mr Cox found these little trips the least taxing of his heavy undertakings, for in his youth he had made many voyages and was very fond of the sea'.

Newberry Cox was also noted for his honesty, which seems to have been another Cox family trait alongside a tendency for manic activity. As Postmaster, Newberry was in a position in which he could stamp an illegal item of mail with the official seal in order to pass it through the postal system. At the time of the American Civil War, a man came ashore from a blockade ship and tried to persuade Newberry to stamp some mail. 'For a fortnight he was entreated to "name his price" – no matter what the amount, and [he] firmly replied that no price could be paid'. It was just as well for Newberry that he resisted temptation as the penalties for dishonesty were severe. A Mr Bethnel Hutchings, who was the Postmaster at Bude Haven in 1846, was convicted of embezzling public money to the value of one penny, and sentenced to seven year's transportation. Happily he received a pardon two years later and was returned to Bude to the delight of friends and neighbours. In a final comment before retiring, Newberry recorded in his notebook the fact that he 'felt that he had had his full share of hard work'.

Fritz knew Newberry Cox as a familiar Falmouth character, but his closest links with the Cox family were with those members involved in the engineering works and the docks. After setting up the chandlers and establishing the engineering works, both Joseph Goodenough and Henry Herbert Cox had married and settled in Falmouth to bring up their own families. Joseph's son Walter, who was a qualified engineer, was only a few years older than Fritz, and along with his wife Ethel, became lifelong friends of Fritz and May. Walter's younger brother Alfred was the same age as Fritz and was probably Fritz's closest friend in Falmouth, as well as being his work colleague and ultimately his boss.

An intriguing connection was made between the Fox and Cox families, not primarily through business, but because of love. A certain Nathaniel Fox was born in Falmouth in 1835, the son of Dr Joseph Fox and his wife Anna Tregelles. Nathaniel was a man who seems to have been determined to make his own way in life, or perhaps he had little alternative as doctors were not necessarily well paid. At the age of sixteen, Nathaniel was employed as an assistant in a chemist's shop in Falmouth, bringing him into daily contact with other businesses in the town where he cannot have failed to notice the rapid growth of James Blatch Cox's ironmongers. It seems that he also noticed James's daughter Elizabeth, who worked in the shop and was the same age as Nathaniel. In September 1857 the Cox and Fox families were linked through the marriage of Elizabeth and Nathaniel in Webber Street Baptist Chapel, conducted by the minister, John Walcot, who had just arrived in Falmouth from York. The wedding service conjures up an interesting picture of Baptist Coxes joining with Quaker Foxes to celebrate the nuptials, with no doubt some thoughts as to how these affairs of the heart might well influence and improve the affairs of business. As it happened the joint energies of Nathaniel and Elizabeth were irresistible and soon Nathaniel Fox was well established as an ironmonger under his own name specializing in the sale of lawnmowers to middle-class ladies. By the beginning of the twentieth century Nathaniel's business was doing well and the census records that his sisters Gertrude and Catherine were 'ironmongers' in their own right and living over the shop at 41 Market Street.

The Foxes and the Coxes shared a common interest in local politics, accompanied by a remarkable ability to achieve recognition quickly and at an early age. Nathaniel's father, Joseph Fox, became Mayor of Falmouth in 1842 at the respectable age of forty-six while James Blatch Cox first became Mayor four years later at the same age, and then again in 1854 when he was in his mid fifties. Nathaniel Fox followed his father in the role of Mayor in 1865 at the age of thirty at much the same sort of age that James's grandson Alfred

Advertisement for Nathaniel Fox's
ironmonger's business.

became Mayor in 1907 at the age of thirty-five. The combination
of business with local politics served both families well, although
religion also had an important part to play. James Blatch Cox had
ceased to be the minister of a congregation, but the family remained
keen Baptists and played their part in the sometimes stormy
evolution of the church in Falmouth. In the late eighteenth century
Cornish Baptists seem to have been viewed with some reservation
by their brothers and sisters in London, and two ministers, William
Steadman and Philip Saffrey, were sent to Cornwall in 1796 by the
Baptist Missionary Society who 'while seeking the good of the
heathen abroad' felt concerned to do something 'for a kind of
character at home, who, though they sustain the Christian name,
yet are heathens in reality, nearly as much as the inhabitants of India
and Africa'. Cornwall was chosen as a promising first sphere of

missionary work among the heathen at home![17] Falmouth Baptists began by meeting in a private house before they established a church in Webber Street that served them well until the 1870s when they were growing in number and needing a larger place in which to meet. Funds were raised, with a surprising major contribution from a Bristol brewer, which enabled Emmanuel Chapel to be built on Market Street on the site of what had been Roskilly's timber yard and carpenters shop, where Packet captains had brought pieces of unusual wood from abroad to be made into ornaments and furniture for their homes. The craftsmen from Roskilly's were involved in the furnishings of the new chapel and were particularly noted for the carving of the gallery, which was made with timber from old ships' masts, and was so remarkable that visitors came from some distance especially to see it. The leading craftsman was a Mr Sampson who had the distinction of not only being a highly skilled worker in wood but was reputed to be the last man in Falmouth to have been taken by the press gang. The driving force behind the new building was the Reverend William Fuller Gooch from Diss in Norfolk, who had been instrumental in the revival of Baptist fortunes in the town, and had single-handedly caused the need for a larger church. Mr Fuller Gooch's enthusiasm was such that the Market Street Chapel was built to accommodate 950 people and subsequently proved to be a huge white elephant, to be replaced eventually in 1939 by new premises on Western Terrace.

Business, politics and religion all had their place as the Foxes, Coxes and Freemans all worked to develop their businesses at a time when Cornwall badly needed a stronger economy. There was however no new golden age because shipbuilding, granite and the business of the port all had to fight against competition from elsewhere, but without these families Cornwall would have been much worse off, and Falmouth would have developed far more slowly. Cornwall's future in the 1880s, when Arthur moved his family to Melvill Road, was uncertain to say the very least, as the crash of the copper price in the 1860s had been followed by the decline of tin in the 1870s and then the general economic downturn of the

[17] L A Fereday, *The Story of Falmouth Baptists*

1880s and 90s. Even the fishing industry was under pressure as pilchards deserted Cornish shores and boats from other parts of England came into Cornish waters with new types of fishing gear, and fewer reservations about working on Sundays. The frustration and anger boiled over in May 1896 when fishermen in Newlyn rose up and destroyed the entire catch of some 100,000 mackerel landed by Lowestoft boats, and it took 350 soldiers and three naval gunboats in Mount's Bay to restore order.

Much of the detail of this period in Cornish history is only now being rediscovered through the work of the Institute of Cornish Studies, which has itself triggered a wider interest in Cornwall's past. Many families played their part in that history and many of those finally settled abroad and have left a Cornish legacy that thrives now and will continue into the future. The Foxes, Coxes and Freemans were examples of a much larger body of people, but it was these three families who were to figure most prominently in Fritz's life as he grew up in the town, which had in so many ways been shaped by them.

Chapter 3

FALMOUTH HAVEN

The move to 8 Melvill Road was a new beginning for the Lewis family, although the house was tightly packed with five boys aged from seven to twenty-two, a girl of nine, and a young woman of twenty besides their father Arthur and a servant. A new regime was needed, and it was Fritz's eldest sister Kate, along with the servant Fianna Hansen from Norway, who organized the household and restored a sense of a secure home, particularly for the younger children. Kate quickly became something of a second mother to the younger ones, and Fritz came to rely on her throughout his life and she enjoyed both his trust and his affection. He would write to her from China at least once a week, and it would be Kate who would look after his interests at home when he was away. Norah, who was two years older than Fritz, was also very close to Kate, and since she never married, she made her home with Kate and her husband for much of the rest of her life.

As Kate gently adjusted the family to their new surroundings, her father also needed to find a new life for himself. Arthur liked to have his family around him and even more so after Ellen died. His children seem to have been content to stay with him, even the older boys, who did not finally leave home until they were married. As a doctor, Arthur's standing in the social order and his professional experience were soon in demand as local communities were required to take on more direct responsibility for their poorest members. The care of the poor was one of the responsibilities of the parish vestry meeting, until the Poor Law Amendment Act of 1834, which aimed to extend central control over parish provisions, and shifted their functions to an elected Board of Guardians, which would administer the provisions of the Act. The idea behind the Act was to bring parishes together into 'unions', which would each have a central place where a workhouse could be built, within reasonable reach of all the parishes, and to that end thirteen unions were set up in Cornwall in 1837. Workhouses were intended to be places where inmates would find less favourable conditions than in employment outside, and in Cornwall, where mining and a life at sea could hardly be described as 'favourable' by any standards, the workhouse was a formidable alternative. Things were made worse by the fact that the regulations under the Act made no concession for situations in which there simply was no employment, as happened in Cornwall on a seasonal or temporary basis because of the nature of the main industries of agriculture, mining and fishing. A dramatic example of the limitation of the regulations was demonstrated when the Mount's Bay fleet was not able to put to sea for some weeks, with the result that 800 men had applied for relief, and technically should have all been removed to the workhouse.[1] Such situations underlined the need for people with local knowledge to administer welfare, and there is some evidence that Guardians in Cornwall tried to interpret the rules as sympathetically as they could, although they also needed to keep the local ratepayers reasonably satisfied. A particular issue surrounded the provision of out-relief, which had been given under the old system to able-bodied paupers in their own homes, but which was savagely discouraged under the new arrangements, and controlled by the Outdoor Relief Prohibitory Order of 1844 which placed draconian restrictions on the Board of Guardians. In Cornwall the Guardians seem to have made the most of the lack of

[1] Peter Tremewan, *The Relief of Poverty in Cornwall 1780-1881*, *Cornish Studies 16.*

any definition in the Act of 'able-bodied', which allowed enough room in interpretation for relief to be given in cases which they astutely described as 'temporary incapacity'. Evidence suggests, that despite the Act of 1834, there was very little change in the ways in which relief was given to the poor in Cornwall before and after 1834, despite the declared intentions of the Act.[2]

The Falmouth Board of Guardians was a respected body of men, and it says much about how Arthur was generally regarded that he was elected to the Board soon after arriving in the town. In April 1890, Arthur was proposed as one of two candidates to be vice-Chairman of the Board, but judiciously withdrew so as not to trigger a vote, and was subsequently appointed as a member of the Visiting Committee, and also the Assessment Committee for the workhouse, which involved vetting people for entry and making sure that the proper facilities were provided. As a doctor, Arthur had a particular interest in the medical provisions, which at that time left a lot to be desired. The problem was not uncommon, and in the mid 1890s, the British Medical Journal (BMJ) visited a number of workhouse infirmaries as part of a campaign to improve nursing and medical care throughout the country. The visitors came to Falmouth in 1894 and were impressed by the position of the workhouse, on high ground, near what is now Union Corner at the junction of Union Road and Trescobeas Road, about a mile and a half from the centre of the town. They commented with approval on the infirmary wards with their pictures on the walls, the bedding of straw or flock, with a few feather beds kept for old people, and the 'rooms small, resembling those in Cornish cottages [that] gives a home-like aspect to the infirmary, and doubtless the patients were, as they said, quite comfortable'. The BMJ group was less impressed by the fact that the regular staffing consisted of one untrained nurse who also acted as midwife when required, 'having been instructed by the doctor in the duties of the post'. If a doctor was needed in an emergency, then he had to be summoned from over a mile away in the town, by a messenger on foot. Despite the grim workhouse buildings, the photographs of which are disturbing to present-day

---

[2] *Cornish Studies 16*, Ed. Philip Payton, p.83.

eyes, the visitors recorded that the diet for the inmates consisted of boiled and roast mutton and beef, stewed meat and broth, with extra milk given out for the night if ordered by the doctor. The matron said that the inmates were also free to roam over the grounds and that seats had been placed for them under the trees, and it is still possible to appreciate what the garden areas were like, despite the fact that the whole site is now derelict, the buildings having been burnt down in 2009. The final report[3] recognized that those in the infirmary were kindly treated but that there was a total absence of any kind of real nursing, and the main recommendation was that the Guardians should build a new hospital which could be properly staffed day and night, and this was eventually done in 1897 at a cost of £2,000, although not before Arthur had to resign as a Guardian due to advancing age. The inquiry did not comment on the rest of the establishment, but at a time when there were questions being raised at a national level about workhouse conditions, there is some evidence that the Falmouth Guardians were maintaining a reasonable standard of care.

The Board met at the workhouse on a fortnightly basis to review what had been happening in the previous two weeks, and to check how many inmates were living there, and how many paupers had been admitted and vagrants relieved. In February 1890 there were 128 people in residence and twenty-four children requiring care, two of which were receiving industrial training. The living arrangements for all the children were the responsibility of the Ladies Boarding Out Committee, which was pressing at the time for an increased allowance per child. The current rate was 3s 2d (£9.48 today) to cover food, clothing and schooling, of which the schooling accounted for the 2d. An increase of 6d (£1.50 today) per week was agreed, with strong support from Arthur, who was well aware of the cost of a family even though he was in a very different financial position. Arthur's voice comes clearly through the otherwise dry verbatim reports which ran in the newspapers each week, and when a question was raised as to whether a particular doctor had prescribed too generous an allowance of meat for a poor sick widow,

---

[3] *BMJ Reports on Nursing and Administration of Provincial Workhouses and Infirmaries 1894-5*

it was Arthur who cut the discussion short by saying that the committee simply did not have power to overrule a doctor. He could be equally determined that professional people, including doctors, did not get away with anything, and when a Dr Rogers from Constantine offered to attend a poor settlement on one day a week for a substantial fee, it was Arthur who pointed out the folly of accepting the proposal, and added that it would be a strange state of affairs if people were only ill enough for a doctor on one fixed day each week.

Arthur's interest in welfare provision was not confined to his formal role with the Guardians. The Falmouth Soup Kitchen was an established charity with a body of subscribers providing funds for soup and bread to be distributed to poor people in winter. In 1890 Arthur was treasurer, and reported to a meeting of supporters that the delivery of soup had started at the beginning of December in the previous year, and then continued to the end of March. The kitchen had given out 4,400 pints of soup (550 gallons) and 2,914 loaves, at a total cost of £70 1s 3d (£4,169) which was less than the previous year's expenditure of £76 10s 9d because the weather had been milder. At the end of the meeting Arthur was thanked for his work as treasurer and was unanimously elected as president.

Arthur's involvement with the Guardians and the soup kitchen is some indication of the energy which he put into care for people at the poorer end of the social scale, and he could have done all that as a public spirited person, without having the exposure that came with public office. Arthur was however, not a person who was afraid to be in the public eye, and he was not one to shirk a responsibility, even if it was of considerable media interest and a cause for regular public complaint. By the time the family moved to Melvill Road he was Chairman of the Urban Sanitary Authority, which was the body that was set up after the Public Inquiry of 1854. The importance of the Sanitary Authority can be gauged by the fact that the board met every three weeks, and among its members was George Henry Fox. It is interesting that membership of the board also included Joseph Goodenough Cox, who was to succeed his father, James, as the Manager of the Waterworks, which was the body with which the

Sanitary Authority did battle on an almost daily basis. The ability of members of the Cox family to be in strategic positions at the most appropriate times is quite breathtaking. The *Falmouth Packet* carried what amounted to a regular column on sewerage and the state of the water supply, and was not slow to castigate the Guardians if it felt that they were falling short in their responsibilities. There was never any shortage of complaints, and a particular source of irritation continued to be the state of the storage pits for the sewers next to Market Street with an outflow into the harbour, which had been raised as in issue thirty-five years earlier at the 1854 Inquiry, but was clearly still a serious problem. The water supply had its own regular column, and complaints ranged from the purity of the water to its availability to the fire brigade through hydrants. After one serious fire, when the nearest hydrant provided no water at all, the Guardians pressed the waterworks manager Joseph Cox for more and better hydrants, which Mr Cox quoted at forty shillings each exclusive of fixing.[4]

The picture of Arthur which comes through the rather impersonal newspaper reports of the Guardians and the other bodies with which he was involved, is of a man who had a sharp sense of humour and a keen sense of justice. He was sufficiently respected for his opinions to sway other members, and it was his incisive interventions that frequently closed discussion, and resulted on the whole in humane decisions. Arthur was a man to have on one's side, and something of his style of humour coupled with a sense of fair play, was inherited by Fritz who was similar to Arthur in that he did not tolerate fools, neither would he give in to bullies nor defer to people who stood on their dignity.

Even before the move from Norway, Fritz's eldest brother Joseph had already left home and was established in Sheffield as an accountant, working in the growing steel cutlery business. He seems to have been rather different from the rest of the family perhaps because, as the eldest, he left home first and wanted to make a different kind of life for himself. Joseph's skill was to manage money

---

[4] *Falmouth Packet*, 8th March 1890.

and before long he had established himself as a company accountant and a trusted figure in a company founded by John Eames of Sheffield. In due course, Joseph would not only marry and settle in the north, but would enable two of Fritz's other brothers, Charles and Walter, to make a permanent move from Falmouth to settle in Sheffield and join the Eames's company.

As they grew up, Arthur's children, apart from Joseph and Fritz, seem to have formed natural pairs, and a bond was developing between Ernest and Harold who were setting their sights on careers at sea. In 1884, when Ernest was twenty-seven, he obtained his certificate of competency as a master mariner, after working at sea for some years. The following year, on the strength of his new status, Ernest proposed to Amelia Gosling, the daughter of a Falmouth shipwright, and they married and settled in Albany Road and started a family. Ernest was to have a busy life at sea and over the next ten years was first mate on a series of sailing cargo ships, having also qualified for steamers. He worked for Edmund Handcock of Falmouth in the mid 1880s, and then for Richard Beryman Chellew who had set up the Cornwall Steamship Company which introduced the tramp steamers *City of Truro* and the *Duke of Cornwall* on regular runs to the coal ports of Wales. The Chellew line had been started in Truro by William Chellew and his son Richard, operating sailing ships out of Falmouth in the 1870s before moving on into steamers. By 1890, when Ernest started work for them, they owned five ships, including the *Duchess of Cornwall* on which Ernest sailed in May of that year, later travelling to the French and Spanish coast, and further on into the Mediterranean and beyond to the Black Sea. From then on, all Chellew's ships were given names which began with 'Pen' so that they were readily identified as not only belonging to the company, but as being Cornish in origin. Although the Cornish-based shipping lines were proud of being Cornish, it is a telling fact that all the ships on which Ernest sailed, except the *Penwith,* were built in the north-east of England rather than the south-west. The pattern holds to the present day, as A & P which operates the docks as part of the Bailey Group, has its roots in the north-east on the Tyne and Tees, with yards at Hebburn and

Middlesbrough. As time went on, Ernest's voyages took him further afield, down the west coast of Africa and latterly to the east coast of the United States. His last employer was Hunting and Pattison, which like the Chellew family, had started with sailing ships in 1874, but by the time that Ernest joined the company, had invested in oil tankers and became a tanker broker and a leading supplier to the oil and gas industry.

Despite the fact that Cornwall was going through a tricky period economically, it is significant that several of the ships on which Ernest sailed were very new. The first ship on which he was first mate, the *Yedmandale*, was only a few months old, and the *Duchess of Cornwall* and the *Pendarves* owned by Chellew's, had both only had one trip before Ernest went to sea on them. However, it was the demise of most of Ernest's ships which is the most sobering part of the story. Of the nine ships on which he served between 1884 and 1895, only one, the *Pendarves*, came to a planned end and was broken up at Spezia in 1951, while all the rest were either wrecked or abandoned at sea, apart from the *Duchess of Cornwall* and the *Etherley* which were torpedoed by German submarines in the First World War.

Arthur's third son, Harold, followed Ernest in becoming a Falmouth-based seaman, although his record is less easy to find. Harold appears on a crew list for the *Llandaff City* in 1901, when the ship was owned and operated by Charles Hill and Sons of Bristol. The Hills had followed a similar pattern to the Chellews, starting with a fleet of North American built sailing ships in the West Indies trading under the Blue Star flag. In due course the company replaced its sailing fleet with steamers and formed the Bristol City Line with cargoes going back and forth across the Atlantic to New York. When Harold was working for the company, it had ten modern steamships, including the *Llandaff City* on which Harold sailed in 1901, and the *Exeter City* on which he was a crew member in 1910/11. This leaves a period of over twenty years for which there is little visible sign in the records except for his marriage in 1888 to Ada Thomas, daughter of William 'Eddy' Thomas, a well-known shipwright in Falmouth, who had built up a successful business at his yard, originally located at an inconvenient site to the east of Bar Road. Prior to moving his business to a much better position at Manor Yard, Eddy Thomas had to launch any newly built vessel across Bar Road and down a long slipway into the water. An astonishing example of this feat appeared in the *Falmouth & Penryn Times* for 10th December 1892, towards the end of Fritz's first year at Cox's Engineering Works. Thomas's yard had built a salvage steamer for Mr A G Anderson, who was a diver and salvage contractor working out of Falmouth and Liverpool, and the new ship was 95 feet long with a beam of 18 feet and weighed, without machinery, nearly 150 tons.

> She was built at least 120 or 130 yards from the water's edge, and the task of launching was unusually difficult, and altogether occupied more than a week. The vessel had to be got across the main road leading to the railway station, which was blocked for many hours, during which all vehicular traffic had to be diverted. Having got across the road, some delay was caused by the vessel running off the ways, but she eventually took to the water in a splendid manner. The steamer is to be engined immediately by Cox and Son, Falmouth.[5]

No doubt the workforce at Cox's watched the whole episode with great interest and probably not a little apprehension, in case the hull should be damaged and therefore the installation of engines delayed. In the end, the ship, which was called the *Etna*, was finished complete with underwater electric lights and was eventually auctioned at the town quay three years after she was launched.

Harold and Ada began married life living with Eddy Thomas and his wife, Sarah, at 2 Arwyn Cottages, which was a useful arrangement, particularly for Ada, as Harold was away at sea on a regular basis. Eddy continued his boatbuilding at Manor Yard and began to turn his attention more towards wooden craft, including the conversion of quay punts, though later on, as harbour working

[5] *Falmouth & Penryn Times*, 10th Dec. 1892.

boats became increasingly motorized and less dependent on sail, the yard built some larger motor-powered work boats, including two for the Morrisson family, who would figure later on in Fritz's life. Eventually Eddy Thomas moved his yard to Ponsharden, where Fritz would in due course lodge his boats when the yard was managed by Eddy's son, Bert, and much later on, Fritz's son Wilf would have one of his boats overhauled and repaired there.

In much the same way that Harold and Ernest had found a common interest in the sea and were putting down roots in Falmouth, Fritz's next two brothers, Charles and Walter, found that they shared an interest in business, and it was not long before their eldest brother Joseph had spotted an opportunity for them in Sheffield with the Eames company of which he was by then company secretary and accountant. Now that Ernest and Harold had left home and were away at sea for much of the time, and Charles and Walter had moved north, the Lewis household felt much smaller and quieter, and although it made life considerably simpler for Kate to manage, there was a sense that something that had felt like a robust refuge from the harsh realities of life was beginning to diminish. Kate was in her early twenties and had met the very presentable John McAllister McGill, a young naval architect, who had come down to Falmouth to work for Cox's at the docks, and it was becoming clear that she too would be leaving home before long. In the meantime, the bond between herself and the three youngest children, Fritz, Norah and Ralph was made closer and stronger and she would always be there for them.

Fritz had begun his schooling in Norway where compulsory education had been introduced rather earlier than most countries, but now it was a matter of where he should be sent to continue his studies in Falmouth. Fritz's future wife, May Page, liked to tell her grandchildren how she had spotted Fritz in the playground at the Grammar School, when she was visiting her grandmother Mary Freeman at 18 Wood Lane. In those days the Grammar School was on the corner of Killigrew Street and what was then Upper Brook Street (now the lower part of Trelawney Road), on the site where the Falmouth Marine School now stands. It appears that some worthy gentlemen from Falmouth had been greatly impressed by a school building which they had seen at Stoke Damerel in Devon, now part of Plymouth, and permission was obtained to use the Devonshire plans in Falmouth, and work was to start in 1824 once the tenant on the site could be persuaded to move his sheep. The site earmarked for the school was at that time on the outskirts of the town, adjoining the rapidly expanding Killigrew Street, and it was only after the disaffected farmer had received an inducement of fifty shillings that he finally shifted his flock and work could begin. 'The building, constructed largely of local stone, consisted of a large schoolroom which could be divided into smaller rooms by partitions, a committee room, a matron's room and "suitable offices", (which meant toilets). The frontage was adorned by "Ionic Pillars" and in the rear was an ample school yard sloped towards the old quarry[6].' The school opened its doors in 1825, but within three years was in a desperate plight, and by 1829 there were only two pupils left. However, largely through the determined efforts of the headmaster Reverend J P Bennetts, the school was brought back from the brink, and by 1868 it became Falmouth Grammar School.

All education was privately run before the Education Act of 1902, so there were two rival schools, Falmouth Grammar School and Kimberley School, whose headmaster was the Reverend I B Eade. The headmasters were however 'not on terms of intimate friendship', and the rivalry was reflected by the pupils of the two schools who occasionally met on the streets of Falmouth with predictable results. The *Penryn Advertiser* of 1875 recorded the details of one meeting in delightful detail:

As it was a half holiday Mr Bennetts' boarders were taking their walks abroad, whilst some of Mr Eade's pupils, who live in the town, were also at large. There was a bit of a scrimmage as to who should have the footpath. One of Mr Bennetts' pupils struck one of the opposite faction under the ribs, and the other retaliated by knocking the other's hat off. Then the boy who had struck the first blow attempted to follow up on

[6] *Penryn Advertiser*, March 1875.

his first hit by another; but in mistake struck a boy named Curry, who belongs to Mr Eade's school. Curry, who had a bat in his hand, ran after the lad who had struck him, and aiming at him struck the son of Mr Bennetts across the eye. Mr Bennetts took out a summons against some of Mr Eade's boys which resulted in cross summonses from Mr Eade. The case came before the magistrates Col Tremayne and Major Bull. Solicitors appeared for both sides, but an adjournment was proposed to the Polytechnic Hall, and after a little discussion all summonses were withdrawn. Col Tremayne expressed his satisfaction at this.

The rivalry between the two schools continued until Mr Bennetts finally got the upper hand, and the Falmouth Grammar School put its rival out of business, leaving no other choice of school for Fritz who made his first acquaintance with Trelawney Road, which in the future, would become such very familiar ground. In later life, Fritz claimed that he was aware that he had been spotted by May while he was at school, and he knew who she was because of seeing her at the Baptist Church when she was staying with her grandparents in Falmouth. It was a period when he sensed something of a vacuum in his life, as the Melvill Road house changed from being dominated by a bunch of noisy boys, to being one with just two boys and two girls and a Norwegian servant who was definitely on the side of the girls. Fritz increasingly looked to friends at school and at church for company, and it was this that brought him into contact with three of Joseph Goodenough Cox's sons – Walter, Ernest and Alfred – all of whom would play an important part in his life. Walter and his wife Ethel became stalwart supporters of Fritz and May through various troubles, Ernest was a friend and a work colleague and Alf, who was the same age as Fritz, became one of his closest friends and ultimately his boss at the waterworks. All this would be part of the future, but in the meantime, Fritz's practical streak and his friendship with Alf took him naturally to Cox's foundry and engineering works, and triggered his interest in all things mechanical.

Fritz in his teens, around the time when
he was sent to Australia and before
starting his apprenticeship at Cox's.

Whatever the future might hold, the period of uncertainty continued on through his teenage years and Arthur's solution to the problem was to dispatch Fritz to Australia with £25 'to sort himself out'. It sounds a drastic action in today's terms, but in the 1880s there was continual coming and going to and from Australia, and there are accounts of other men who set off, or were sent off, to try their luck in mining or the newly discovered gold fields. The story in the Lewis family was that Fritz eventually found himself on a sheep farm, which was quite likely, given that the levels of wages in the mines and the lure of the gold fields had drawn many men off the land in Australia and there was a crying need for farm workers. Fritz himself told a number of stories of his time abroad including one, no doubt heavily embroidered yarn, about saving a man from being lynched. Fritz liked to describe how tempers on isolated farms could run high if there was friction between the men, and he arrived at one such place to find a man sitting on his horse, with his hands tied behind his back, and a noose around his neck with the end tied to the branch of a tree. It was quite obvious from the sullen group of horsemen surrounding the man what was afoot, and Fritz asked to know what crime the man had committed. The ringleader of the group volunteered the information that they had all borne as much as they could stand of a man 'who claims to be better educated than the rest of us and who is such an infernal know-all!' In a place where there was no escape from other people's company, things had apparently got so bad that the men had decided to rid themselves of this extremely irritating person. Fritz asked if he might test the man's knowledge to see if his claim to be educated was true or false, and the group of men, who may have started to wonder if they could really go through with their plans, agreed to let him ask some questions provided they could all hear what he said and what answers were given in reply. Fritz chose a Latin phrase which he recited to the man and asked him to translate. The man gave the correct answer, and after one or two further enquiries along similar lines, Fritz declared that the man was indeed as educated as he

Dr Arthur Lewis at about the time that
Fritz began his apprenticeship at
Falmouth Docks

claimed to be. The men reluctantly agreed to remove the rope from the man's neck, and after some forthright warnings, set him free. At this point the man came over to Fritz, and instead of thanking him for saving his life, proceeded to tell him that his Latin pronunciation was appalling! The story always amused Fritz, and it probably got longer and more embroidered each time it was told.

On his return to Falmouth as an older and no doubt much wiser young man, Fritz was ready to sign on for an apprenticeship in marine engineering at Cox and Company. The indenture document was large and impressive and left nothing to doubt. Fritz was to start on 4th January 1892 and his apprenticeship would last until 4th January 1895 which strangely enough would be three years and one day. Fritz was accompanied by his father, Arthur, who under the terms of the agreement, undertook to pay £70 to Cox and Company and to provide 'board and lodging, clothing and all other necessaries during the said term'. The Company for their part undertook to teach Fritz to be a Mechanical Engineer and to 'pay unto him five shillings per week during the said term…'. There would be no pay during any absence for sickness and any time lost would be added on to make up the full term, however there was provision for overtime at tuppence farthing per hour in the afternoon, and six pence per quarter day. The indenture document was signed by Fritz and Arthur on the one hand, and Joseph Goodenough Cox, Henry Herbert Cox, his son Herbert Henry Cox and Walter Reseigh Cox on behalf of Cox and Company, and all this was done in the presence of a witness, a naval architect called John McAllister McGill, who had married Fritz's sister Kate in June of the previous year.

At Cox's, Fritz was one of a number of apprentices, and the day-to-day life of a foundry and engineering works would have gone on in much the same way as it did for the next century, until apprenticeships changed and became something of the past. The relationship between men and boys would have been quite as much part of the total learning experience as the teaching of technical knowledge and skills. All the old jokes would have been played, and boys would have been sent to the foreman 'to ask for a long weight', and found themselves standing around doing exactly that until someone was kind enough to tell them about the joke. Boys would have been sent for 'left-handed spanners' and 'right-handed nuts' until they got to know the look in the joker's eyes, and to identify the men who liked to play tricks. There would be other things which would trigger a round of teasing, and posing for the painter Henry Scott Tuke would have been high on the list, though perhaps Tuke paid them well enough to make it worth their while because he never seemed to be short of volunteers.

The Docks Foundry and Engineering Company had been set up in 1868 by Joseph Goodenough Cox and Henry Herbert Cox to carry out ship repairing and ship breaking. Ten years on, the company began building ships, and by the end of the century was employing between 500 and 600 men constructing small vessels of up to 200 tons, with an occasional vessel of over 300 tons. While Fritz was working at Cox's the larger orders were mainly for tugs, though the company also built smaller boats, among which were ferries and small passenger craft. Cox's was well known for the quality of its work, and a St Mawes company recorded that the *Rosalind*, built by Cox's, was so 'very well constructed and suitably designed, she lasted sixty years eventually being sold to the Falmouth Docks and Engineering Company for a work boat'.[7]

Cox's also built engines which were fitted into vessels constructed by other yards. Probably the most well-known example was the triple-expansion engine fitted to the tug *Victor* built by Pool, Skinner and Williams of Falmouth in 1898 and based in the harbour until 1926, when it was sold on to an owner in Cardiff and then another at Swansea. This solid and dependable tug, which had played such a vital role in the rescue of the crew of the *Ponus* when it was stranded and on fire on Gyllyngvase Beach in 1915, was only finally broken up in 1954.

The day-to-day pattern of activity in the engineering works could be interrupted by events outside the docks, and one such

---

[7] Graham Farr, *West Country Passenger Steamers.*

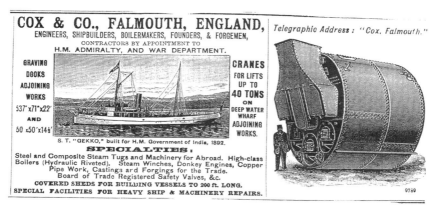

Cox & Co. advertisement.

occasion was reported in the *Falmouth Packet* of 9th January 1892 in the very first week of Fritz's apprenticeship.

> It appears a small engine and boiler were recently bought by Mr Crook, builder who sold it to Mr Rickard, who desired it to work his lathes. The engine was taken to Messrs Cox, engineers, at the Dock Iron Works and fully tested there on Monday. On Tuesday it was taken to the shop, and the boiler placed in position on specially erected brick work. Mr Rickard himself was attending to the boiler and there were several other persons present. Fortunately for these the explosion sent the boiler clean through the roof and fell in Messrs Cox's yard. Had it taken a lateral course loss of life must have inevitably ensued.

A small number of people were hurt but fortunately no one was killed. One of Cox's apprentices called Hewis was hit by flying fragments but was eventually calmed by fellow workers, and the article ended by recording, that though the engine was new, the boiler was an old one, though it had been thoroughly tested, and the injured were progressing satisfactorily. This was not the only drama for Cox's works as it had only recently recovered from a fire which had completely destroyed the joiners and moulders' shed, causing over £1,000 worth of damage, which the *Falmouth Packet* recorded, somewhat surprisingly as 'only partly covered by insurance', unless the paper was having a sly dig at one of Cox's other roles, as an agent for the Norwich Union insurance company. The report went on to say that 'the joiners shop contained a large stock of material, including a quantity of teak fittings for ships, the firm being engaged in building vessels for Havannah, China and Fowey'.[8] In the light of later events, the link between Cox's and China seems to have been well established.

Among the Cox's apprentices Fritz stood out, not least because of his local reputation in the water as a swimmer, and on dry land as a rugby player. Fritz joined the swimming club in his early teens and developed into an accomplished swimmer who could hold his own with anyone in the sea, and could also enter the water from a diving board with a clean slice and no splash. He established himself sufficiently well with the club that when he was only seventeen, he was unanimously elected captain at the 1889 annual meeting, at a time when the club was struggling to survive and needed leadership and encouragement to carry on. One of the clubs most enthusiastic supporters was the artist Henry Scott Tuke, who was a vice-president at the time, and very much aware of Fritz's abilities in the water. In the event, Fritz's captaincy was short-lived because of other things which were happening in his life, and at the annual meeting of the following year the secretary reported that 'during the year several members had left the town, amongst them being our captain Mr Fritz Lewis and also our sub captain; both these friends showed great interest in the club, and we all wish them every success in their new spheres of labour'.[9] The meeting went on to discuss how the club might improve its image and be more attractive to people in the town, and it was agreed that there was a need for 'more important matches' to stimulate interest, and as a means of enthusing the general public, the club had already provided 'bathing appliances' at Gyllyngvase beach, and there was a suggestion, which was rejected, that the annual subscription for adults might be reduced from its current level of 2s 6d and 1s 0d for lads.

---

[8] *Falmouth Packet,* 13th April 1889.
[9] *Falmouth Packet,* 10th May 1890.

Henry Scott Tuke in Falmouth in 1894

That however was not the end of Fritz's swimming career by a very long way, and three years later, when Fritz was in the middle of his apprenticeship at Cox's and swimming better than ever, the *Falmouth Packet* of 22nd April 1893 carried an account of the club's Annual Meeting in which the secretary, Mr R T K Vinson, read a report of the annual grand challenge race.

> The grand challenge race was an excellent one, but as has been the case for the last two or three seasons, Mr Fritz Lewis won. This gentleman is now the undisputed owner of the challenge cup, he having won it in accordance with the regulations laid down viz. two successive times.

At the same Annual Meeting Fritz was elected to the committee of the club, and he not only played his part as a member, but also continued to swim competitively. Two years later he had progressed sufficiently to enter as a competitor in the annual swimming matches organized by the Penzance Swimming Club, which were part of an altogether rather grander occasion than the ones in Falmouth. The event took place on 20th August 1895 in front of the Promenade at Penzance, which was brightly decorated with bunting as backdrop to the town band playing a lively selection of numbers, under the baton of Mr P M Westfield. The weather was fine and bright, although the sea in which the competition would take place was described as being 'a little choppy'. The programme included eleven events, of which the seventh match was for the Amateur Championship of Cornwall, open to competitors born in Cornwall or who were bona fide residents in the county for the two previous years. The first prize was the Gold Medal of the Association, with 'silver salts' for second place and an aneroid for third.

Two newspapers recorded the events of the day, although when it came to the championship match, local loyalties seem to have affected the reporting to such an extent that the accounts might be of two different races. The *Cornish Telegraph* said that there were four competitors although it listed five names; J H Gartrell and Fritz Lewis from Falmouth, John Ward from Truro and T H Trounson and B Beckerlec, although the last-named man was not mentioned again so seems to have dropped out. The paper went on to say that 'the main competition was between Gartrell and Lewis for the first position, but the Falmouth representative rounded the mark first, and maintained the lead. The interest was then centred in the race for second place, Trounson overhauling Gartrell for second place. The time was 8 minutes and 21 seconds'.

The reporter for the *Cornishman* sounded more enthusiastic, though he referred to 'Fitz' rather than Fritz Lewis, and wrote that the championship 'was expected to be a lively and well contested event', and so it proved to be. The race was started by the firing of a gun by Sergeant Instructor Sainsbury, who also fired at the finish to establish the exact time.

Trounson shot to the front with Gartrell at his shoulder, but Fitz [sic] Lewis soon worked into first place. Ward after a very short trial gave up. Gartrell fell behind and swam horizontally near the half buoy which caused him to lose more ground. Trounson and the Falmouth man swam capitally. These two had their heads level and struggled on their merits without seeing each other. Trounson almost caught Fitz Lewis in a final spurt, but the stranger won by a couple of yards, with Gartrell thirty or more yards behind.[10]

The prizes were presented by the Mayor of Penzance, W H Julyan Esq. JP, in the saloon of the committee boat, *The Lady of the Isles* which had been 'tastefully decorated for the occasion'. The ceremony was attended by local dignitaries including Lord Penzance and Lord St Levan from St Michael's Mount, and Fritz received the gold medal, shaped as a shield with cut-out diving figures forming a crest. Considering that a Falmouth man had beaten two Penzance men and one from Truro, it seems surprising that there was no report in the *Falmouth Packet*, but nothing could take anything away from Fritz's triumph, and in later life May loved to produce his medal for his grandchildren to admire.

A painting entitled *By the Committee Boat: Are you Ready?* by W H Bartlett, showing the start of a race during the swimming matches at St Ives in 1895. (courtesy of David Tovey)

Only four days after his triumph at Penzance Fritz was swimming again, but this time at St Ives where he won the Open

---

[10] *The Cornishman*, 22nd August 1895.

Amateur 600-yard race with a prize of an oil painting. He might have preferred the second prize, a telescope, which was won by Kistler, the younger brother of George Kistler who was a world title holder for the mile.[11]

Swimming was not the only sport at which Fritz did well. He played both tennis and cricket, but his favourite game was rugby football which is a sport very close to the Cornish heart. Alongside Cornish wrestling, rugby was a Cornish national institution in which there was hot competition and huge local and county interest, which is re-emerging in the present century. In October 1893, Fritz was selected to play for East Cornwall against West Cornwall, which amounted to a preliminary county trial in which players from Redruth, Truro and Falmouth formed the East team, against players from Penzance, Penryn and Camborne for the West. Following the match, the selectors went on to divide the players into the *Possibles* and the *Probables* and Fritz was selected as a forward for the latter. The scores in the trials were not of as much interest as the decision of the selectors in picking players for the county team, and in December, Fritz found himself as one of two Falmouth players named for the match between Cornwall and Gloucester. The game was hard fought, but Gloucester was a very powerful side who eventually won by two goals and two tries, against nil for the Cornishmen.

When Fritz finished his time at Cox's and qualified as a marine engineer, he seems to have had less time for sport, although he retained sufficient interest and involvement to have been referee for a match in 1895 between Falmouth and Penryn. Given the rivalry between the two towns, Fritz was either a very trusted referee, which may have come about because of having been a county player, or alternatively he was simply tough enough to take control of what would have been a needle match, with no quarter given. Loyalties ran deep, and even the reporters writing in the *Falmouth Packet* found it difficult to conceal where their interests lay, and this applied to the accounts of women's as well as men's competitions. In the present

---

[11] *St Ives Transcrit 1895*, and information from Geoff Swallow.

century there seems to be an assumption that women have only recently received the same attention as men in the media reporting of their sports, and yet the *Falmouth Packet* in the latter part of the nineteenth century, carried full reports of ladies' football and cricket which were not patronizing or lacking in partisan feeling when Falmouth ladies soundly beat Penryn at football. An account of the Falmouth ladies' cricket team versus the Falmouth Grammar School boys described a hard fought game which the ladies eventually won, due to a batting partnership by two of the ladies who 'thrashed the ball all around the ground'. Other towns in Cornwall seem to have lagged well behind Falmouth in providing events for women alongside men. As early as the mid 1880s the town's swimming matches included women's races, whereas it was at least another twenty years before there were women's swimming events at Penzance or St Ives.

The enthusiasm for rugby in Falmouth resulted in there being two clubs — Falmouth Albions and Falmouth RFC — between whom there was understandably very considerable rivalry. The problem was that the town was not big enough to produce a sufficient number of good players for two clubs, and the feeling was robustly expressed in the *Falmouth Packet* of 31st March 1894 that the clubs must combine if Falmouth was ever going to produce a strong enough team to beat arch-rivals like Redruth and Camborne. A decision was finally reached to combine the clubs, starting with the 1894/95 season, but newspaper reports show that separate teams continued to play that year, so some confusion seems to have continued. The aim of improving the quality of play did however take hold, and in September 1894 there was even a match to decide the captaincy of the Falmouth RFC, although the result remained unreported in the *Falmouth Packet*. At about this time, Fritz was made Falmouth skipper, and later newspaper reports refer back to him as having captained the side during a revival of Falmouth's rugby fortunes, but the precise dates are not clear.

Fritz enjoyed his sport, but he was well aware that when he finished at Cox's he would need to face the harsh realities of life at sea, and he had few illusions having heard so many stories from his elder brothers about their lives on board. As Fritz began to contemplate working in China and the South China Sea, he would have been aware of the reputation for highly unpredictable weather in that part of the world, with its typhoon season promising hugely powerful storms. It would be easy to assume that Fritz would only have read accounts of such events at second- or third-hand, were it not for the great storm of 1891. At the time Fritz was nineteen and preparing to begin his apprenticeship at Cox's in the following year, when a hurricane struck Cornwall at midday on Monday 9th March. There seems to have been little warning of the storm and there was certainly not time for ships to make port, although subsequent events showed that even sheltered harbours were no guarantee of safety in the face of such a massive onslaught. The hurricane blew for thirty hours, and even after eighteen hours of storm, it seemed to be getting worse rather than better. No boat in the harbour was safe, and the *Falmouth Packet* listed dozens of owners whose boats had been sunk or smashed to bits.

> Close to the landing piers are the sewage tanks and between them and the stone wall of Mrs Downing's premises is an opening, flanked on one side by the King's Arms and Mr Grose's establishment. This particular spot forms a sort of dock and during the gale on monday night a big sail punt belonging to Mr Tuke, artist, got in there. Later on a large coal hulk belonging to Messrs Vivian and Son broke from her moorings and got into the same place, smashing through the pier and knocking down the substantial wall enclosing Mrs Downing's yard.[12]

At Cox and Co. there was some quick thinking and the new tug *Hercules* was taken up the Penryn River for safety, although the *Victor* was not so lucky, and her bows were smashed in by a collision with another vessel in the harbour. A German steamship went aground in Gerrans Bay beside an English ship which was already a wreck. The four-masted *Bay of Panama* ran onto Penare Point near the entrance to the Helford River and the captain, his wife and

[12] *Falmouth Packet*, 14th March, 1891.

several of the crew were lost. It had not been possible to launch the lifeboat, because any tugs that might have been available were already trying to help steamers. The brig *Crusader* from Caernarvon, carrying slate for Hamburg, was abandoned off Trevose Head with seven feet of water in the hold, but the captain and five crew managed to get off in the ship's boat and despite being tossed around in it for eighteen hours were eventually landed by the fishing smack *Gratitude*, although by that time one of the crew members had not surprisingly died. The harbour and bay were littered with wrecks, with the steamer *Dundela* ashore at Portloe, the *Carl Hirschberg* on rocks at Porthscatho and the *Helen* of the Coverack Stone Company ashore on Castle Point at St Mawes. In Falmouth itself several elms along the rope walk had been uprooted by the wind and a hundred feet of sea wall by the Falmouth Hotel had been demolished.

By Wednesday 11th March the storm had blown itself out, there was not a cloud in the sky and the sea was as still as a millpond, although 'a pea soup mist hung over the harbour'. The scene of devastation would have imprinted itself on the young Fritz as a taste of what extreme weather could do, and he would know that typhoons on the Chinese coast were far stronger and more frequent than hurricanes in Cornwall. He did not know however, that the typhoon which would hit Hong Kong on 18th September 1906 during his time in China, would make the Cornish hurricane seem mild in comparison.

As his apprenticeship at Cox's came to an end, Fritz turned his attention to what was now going to be his occupation and main source of income for the foreseeable future, and a series of trips followed as an engineer on different ships, as he gained more experience. In December 1897 he joined the steam yacht *Roseneath* which was setting out from Cowes for an extensive cruise around the Mediterranean, although she was delayed for some time in Falmouth because of very bad weather, and did not pass Gibraltar until the middle of January. The ship, which had been built by Day Summers & Co. in 1875, belonged to a period when steam and sails could be used together. If the sea was rough, the sails were sometimes set on the *Roseneath* to enable the ship to progress, with the engines running slow, so that they did not race excessively if the propeller came clear of the water. The engineer's job was exacting, and although the engines worked well on the whole, they required constant monitoring and adjustment, and occasionally they had to be stopped altogether and stripped down to cure problems with bearings or condensers.

The itinerary depended on the whim of the owner and so the ship went back and forth around Marseilles, Cannes and Monaco before continuing on via Naples, Capri and a host of other ports until it reached Trieste in June. Fritz saw to the polishing of brass and the manning of the launch, as well as loading vast quantities of Welsh or Newcastle coal whenever the ship was in port for long enough. The boilers burnt anything up to three tons every twenty-four hours unless the sails were in use, and supplies had to be loaded without covering the owner and his friends in clouds of coal dust. Fritz was required to keep a log of the voyage, with notes about coal consumption and the performance of the engines, but when the ship moored in Marseilles and the fabulously rich Prince Adam Czartoryski came on board, Fritz could not resist making a note of it alongside the need for a fitter for the slide valves. This log was perhaps the forerunner of the diaries that he would keep in a few years time, which would record the details of engines and weather, but would also paint a picture of life at sea and the characters who sailed on his ships.

All was going well for Fritz in the Adriatic, but the same could not be said for life in Falmouth as Arthur's health, at the age of eighty-one, began to deteriorate. A message was telegraphed to the *Roseneath* in Trieste requesting Fritz's immediate return home, and so he signed off the ship on 7th June and took the fastest passage he could find back to Cornwall, arriving with a few days to spare before his father died.

On 21st June Arthur Lewis slipped away peacefully at his house overlooking Kimberley Park, and his family gathered in Falmouth to mourn his passing and lay him to rest next to Ellen in

Fritz at about the time of his
father's death in 1898.

the cemetery above Swanpool. Ernest, Walter and Fritz were joined by Norah and Kate, who was now Mrs McGill. Harold was away at sea but his wife Ada joined her sisters-in-law at the funeral, and Joseph and Fanny sent a wreath from Sheffield. Alf Cox and Herbert Henry Cox represented the Cox family and flowers were sent from 'All at Lanarth'. The *Falmouth Packet* carried a report of Arthur's funeral:

> Dr A Lewis, one of the oldest inhabitants of Falmouth, passed away this week at the age of 81. The deceased was well known throughout the county and was highly respected by the inhabitants of the town. For some years [he was] a member of the Falmouth Board of Guardians and Chairman of the House Committee. He was also Chairman of the old Parish Local Board for some years and a member of the Sewerage Board.[13]

Arthur had achieved what he had set out to do in bringing his family from Norway to Cornwall and supporting them as they made

---

[13] *Falmouth Packet*, June 1898.

their own ways in life and started their own families. After Ellen died, his house had been home to his unruly boys who were quietly but firmly managed by Kate, with the help of Norah and their Norwegian servant. Fritz had felt secure in the bosom of his family and his experience of family life was one that he wanted to replicate, and he now knew in his own mind with whom it was that he wanted to share his life in the future.

PART THREE

CHINA

Chapter 4

CORNWALL to CANTON

Why does a young man of thirty-two, who is settled in the family home in Falmouth and engaged to the love of his life, decide to up sticks in 1904 and go to work in China?

At first sight it seems an odd thing to do, and especially if there is an assumption that Cornwall's population was static and not particularly adventurous in the latter part of the nineteenth century. A great deal has been written about the decline in mining and the changes in the internal economy of Cornwall, but until recently there seems to have been less awareness of the emigration from the county from as early as 1815, which gathered pace in the 1840s with the potato famine, and then grew rapidly in the 1860s and 70s as the economic downturn was exacerbated by the crash in the world market price for copper. The fact is, that the Cornish have had a tradition for being on the move because of the sheer necessity of finding the next viable source of income in an area where there has been a steady fight for financial survival by the majority of ordinary people. In the early eighteenth century, the population gravitated to the industrial districts of Gwennap and Camborne-Redruth, but as further discoveries of copper were made further east, so miners and their families followed, moving around Cornwall in pursuit of available work. Cornish people seem to have become accustomed to being mobile, and while some moved further into England, and particularly to the lead mines of Wales, the majority looked further afield abroad. Proximity to the sea and news of discoveries overseas led many Cornish people to emigrate to Canada, America, South Africa and Australia. As early as the 1830s and 40s news and information flowed back from these countries to Cornwall and newspapers carried news of what had happened to emigrants with details of where they had gone and how they were doing. In many places Cornish associations were established which meant that a new arrival in Canada or Australia would quickly discover fellow countrymen ready to help find somewhere to live and work. The Cornish were often pioneers in setting up trade unions, and overseas branches of the Freemasons and Oddfellows provided new settlers with assistance. In the earlier part of the nineteenth century whole families set off to find a better life, while later in the century it tended to be the men, and particularly the younger men who went abroad. Philip Payton, the Director of the Institute of Cornish Studies, has drawn attention to the alarming statistics 'which show how Cornwall was robbed of the younger, more energetic and better trained elements of its population. Between 1861 and 1900, 44.8 per cent of the Cornish male population aged 15 to 24 had left for overseas, with a further 29.7 per cent leaving for other counties.'[1]

The Cornish led the world in the skills and equipment required for hard-rock mining and Cornish miners were the first to be recruited by new mining enterprises overseas. Cornish engines were shipped to Mexico from Harvey & Co. of Hayle, and as late as 1908 a large engine contract worth £5,500 was completed by Holman's of Camborne for the La Blanca mine at Pachuca in Mexico. The demise of copper mining in Cornwall meant that there were second-hand engines lying idle and overseas agents were quick to realize the value in purchasing used machinery. In 1847 the directors of the Burra mine in South Australia wrote to John Bibby & Sons of Liverpool asking them to procure a second-hand steam

---

[1] Philip Payton, *The Cornish Overseas*, p.28.

engine as used in Cornish mines. There are numerous accounts of new and used machines being shipped out from Cornwall to new mine workings, together with descriptions of the huge effort required to get heavy metal parts ashore and dragged over inhospitable terrain to remote mining areas.

It is hard now to grasp the degree to which men, often with their families, travelled across the world in pursuit of work and were so keenly sought after and welcomed by mining businesses. In his book, *The Cornish Overseas,* Philip Payton traces the great emigration in detail and gives many examples, among which is the career of William John Oates, who was born in Cornwall in 1859 and worked as a youth at Wheal Unity Wood near Chacewater before travelling to his first 'real' job at a silver mine in Peru, run by his uncle. From there he went to Bolivia before returning to Cornwall in 1887 to marry. After the birth of a daughter in 1888 he set off to Uruguay where he became 'captain' of the Hermanos Goldfields Mining Co. Ltd. William's wife joined him in South America in 1889, but by 1891, they were back in Cornwall, although within the year he was off back to Peru for a second, and later, a third term. Back in Cornwall again in 1897, William was soon in demand to advise on gold mining enterprises in the Ural Mountains in Russia from where he moved on to Southern Rhodesia and Matabeleland. By 1902 William was working with silver mines in Mexico before going back to South America, then to County Cork in Ireland, before ending up with a last trip to Peru followed by Malaya and Argentina. He finally retired back to Cornwall and died at Lostwithiel in 1935. The Cornish overseas naturally kept together and formed ex-patriot communities, but frequently they became naturalized and went on to be leading people in the wider national scene. There are accounts of Cornishmen becoming successful businessmen as well as judges and district governors. Cornish wrestlers established a feared reputation in various parts of the world, and in 1903, it was said that the Mexican national football team was composed entirely of Cornishmen. Nearer home to Fritz were the Pengilly sisters who were his near neighbours at Brook House on Trelawney Road in Falmouth, all three of whom had been born in Mexico, daughters of a well-known mine captain who left them sufficiently well provided for that they were living on private means without any need to seek other income. Thomas Pengilly had died at Pachuca in Mexico in 1893 where his small son Thomas Alvino had also died five years earlier aged four. Thomas's wife, Elizabeth, who originally came from the mining district of Gwennap, had to pack up the family and bring her daughters back to Falmouth in much the same way as other Cornish people had to come back from overseas mine workings, though not always in quite such sad but well-funded circumstances.

Against this background of the huge emigration from Cornwall to find work, Fritz's decision to go abroad to earn a living does not seem quite so strange. He most probably heard about the job in China through Cox's Engineering Works which was building gunboats for service in China at the time, and like Fox's shipping agents, were often used by overseas businesses when they needed to recruit reliable employees. There are no hints in his diaries to suggest what was in his mind at the time, but Fritz was a man who thought carefully about the future and made detailed preparations for it. He realized that he needed to increase his income if he was going to give himself the chance of saving, and he knew that he would be able to earn more overseas than at home. His starting pay in Hong Kong dollars would have been equivalent, at the time, to about £22 per month which was a level that he did not achieve in England until about ten years later in 1918. Once he was in China he saved every spare cent, as is witnessed by the fact that out of his monthly pay of between $200 and $240 he regularly put away all but about $20, added to which his food and board were provided on the ship, which represented a significant hidden bonus. He kept in close contact with the Hong Kong and Shanghai Banking Company, and he was in touch with his family and agents back home in England arranging the purchase of shares, and as he prepared to leave China in 1908, he bought gold. These were the actions of a man who was seeking to establish a strong financial base on which he could build. It was the passion of a man, who not only kept minute accounts of everything including a record of tips to waiters, but a man who had

John Freeman, who was the founding force behind Freeman and
Sons Granite, and his wife Mary Deane, who continued to live
in Wood Lane with her daughters after John died in 1874.

a bigger vision in mind as he wrote twice or three times a week to
May Page, the woman whom he was determined to marry in the
course of time. Fritz purposely decided to take on the very evident
risks of foreign travel, and working in an often dangerous
environment, in order to be able to marry and support May in the
custom to which he felt she was entitled, though she would have
gladly settled just for being with him no matter what. In the back of
his mind he would have been very much aware of the financial
solidity of the Freemans, living in Wood Lane in Falmouth, who
would hope and expect that a granddaughter and niece would be
well provided for. Mary Freeman, the elderly widow of John
Freeman the force behind Freeman Granite, presided over the
household of her remaining unmarried daughters, who not only
doted on May, but seem to have been very fond of the young Fritz
and were very supportive of the idea of an engagement. Fritz wrote
from China to May's aunts, Alice and Sophie, and they in turn wrote
to him. Later on he visited them regularly in Wood Lane and
remembered their birthdays, as they remembered his.

The earliest of Fritz's surviving diaries is the one for 1905, and it contains very little about what he was thinking and feeling as he made his preparations to travel to China, but he had to make some important choices about what to take and what to leave behind. It is clear that he was travelling to take on a particular job, because his passage had been arranged so that he would be in Hong Kong by the end of the year, and ready to start work in January. Most probably he was expecting to be there for up to five years, thousands of miles away on the other side of the world, in a completely unfamiliar setting, so he went well armed with two or three revolvers, an air rifle and at least one shotgun. Perhaps his previous experiences in Australia had taught him to be prepared for trouble, and although he sold two of his revolvers quite soon after arriving, he had reason to be glad of his armoury, partly for shooting birds. but not least for dealing with more than one attack from pirates.

Fritz writes to May from the *SS Palawan* during a rough passage down the English Channel

Fritz set sail from London on 27th October 1904 on the *Palawan,* a P&O passenger ship of 4,500 tons, carrying 65 adults and 7 children to destinations in the Far East. The first day of the voyage was not promising, as Fritz recorded on a picture postcard of the ship which he sent to May with the message 'As the Pilot is going ashore at the Isle of Wight I take this opportunity to drop you a line to let you know that I am alright. Half an hour ago we took some water on board and we had a drenching in our cabin, some of my things got wet but I was up on deck so escaped it.' As May contemplated five years of separation from Fritz and worried about his safety, she would have found little comfort in his card and the description of his things being soaked by the sea before the ship had even left the English Channel! The card was addressed to May at 3 Derwentwater Mansions in Acton where she was coming to terms with other changes in her life. She had nursed her mother, Sarah, through three debilitating years with bowel cancer before she finally died three months before Fritz sailed. While her mother was ill her father William Page, who was a Baptist minister, had been accepted for ordination in the Church of England by the Bishop of London, and had been made deacon in 1902 and then priest in 1903. At the same time as Fritz was setting off to China, William had been told that he was about to be offered the living of Chilcompton in Somerset by the Bishop of Bath and Wells. Meanwhile May was coping with the loss of her mother, the departure of Fritz and the prospect of a move away from her friends in London in the company of her rather humourless and demanding father.

May was one of those people who dealt with the pressures of life by finding a new occupation, and she decided that she would follow Fritz's progress by carefully collecting his postcards which arrived in a steady stream. In March, Fritz bought three ornate Japanese postcard albums with lacquered covers in deep red, embossed with a romantic image of a man punting his wife in a golden boat towards an enchanted island. The albums cost $3.75, and when Fritz posted them off to May he placed a picture of a geisha girl inside the first album, with a slightly heavy commentary on the back which played on the word 'May':

To my dear <u>May</u>,

Trusting your birthday <u>may</u> be a very happy one. This [the geisha picture] will also do to put in your album and I was afraid to spoil it by sending through the post. Some people <u>may</u> admire the picture on the other side but I am afraid it is not much to my taste. I much prefer an English face and like it so much that I have already written it three times. Here's a puzzle for you from yours ever,

    F.L.

It is as close a Fritz comes to recording his intimate feelings but there is no doubt that he missed May very much and wanted to be with her, but any allusions to the sexual aspects of their relationship does not come through the diaries, even much later when they are on honeymoon. The Chinese euphemism for sex – 'clouds and rain' – may have summed up Fritz's philosophical view of things as he contemplated the huge geographical distance between himself and May, and the length of time before they would see each other again.

Postcards continued to arrive at Acton, and May was able to follow the progress of the *Palawan* calling at Malta before reaching Port Said on 29th November. Fritz sent 'best wishes for Xmas and New Year' and the card shows the entrance to the Suez Canal with some intriguing naval sailing ships that had been converted to steam, with a single narrow funnel set centrally and contrasting oddly with the huge masts and spars.

The ships are a reminder of the fact that Fritz was living in a time of significant change as navies were beginning to come to terms with the transition from wooden sailing ships to steam-driven steel hulls. The ships in the postcard picture would have been from the period before the move to iron hulls when the British and French were converting wooden battleships to steam, and even building wooden ships from scratch to be powered by the new steam engines. It must have been strange to see naval craft in the Mediterranean in 1904 which were not very different from their forbears which fought

A postcard of Port Said showing a sailing ship (left foreground) that has been converted to steam, with a funnel amidships.

at Trafalgar a century earlier. It would be less than a year later, in 1905, that Fritz would record news of the sinking of a Russian fleet by the Japanese, who had equipped themselves with a state-of-the-art navy constructed entirely of steel.

Since Fritz was travelling on a P&O ship, the passage through the Suez Canal would have been a memorable experience. Long before the canal was even contemplated, P&O had sailed to Port Said with passengers and mail and had conducted them in some luxury overland to Suez, to be taken aboard another P&O ship which would carry them onwards to the East. The company was well used to ensuring a speedy and safe transfer and was slow to take on board how much difference the Canal would make to sea travel to the Far East. The building of the Suez Canal shortened the route to China by 3,000 miles, but its opening triggered a mixture of reactions and also generated some slightly surprising results.

Some shipping lines were suspicious of the new canal and assumed that it was not going to work. P&O was so sure that the canal would not be of benefit to the company that, even while it was being constructed, the company carried on building ships which required too great a depth of water to be able to go through it. When the company subsequently realized its mistake, it had to sell at a loss about 40,000 tons of their older vessels which were fit for several years work, and at the same time it was necessary to build upwards of 80,000 tons of new ships.[2] For the first two years after the canal was open to shipping P&O's income fell by £100,000 per annum and it could not pay a dividend. The problem for P&O was not simply to do with revenue but the fact that the company had large overheads from having pioneered passenger and mail routes to the Far East, and had built docks and warehouses in Egypt, where it also maintained lighters and coal dumps. Although the advent of the steamer age was widely trumpeted, the new ships required vast quantities of coal, which was simply not available in sufficient bulk east of Suez. In order to keep its fifty steamships at sea, P&O had to establish fourteen coaling stations which were kept supplied by no less than 170 sailing colliers. The company had also established fruit, vegetable and sheep farms to feed passengers in transit, as well as having steamers on the Nile and camels for overland transport. It was said that the P&O ship's stores in Egypt stocked everything from needles to anchors, and even the lighthouses down the length of the Red Sea that everyone used, were built and manned by P&O. The company's directors continued to assume that business would continue as usual, with passengers and mail going overland past Suez, as it always had done.

The Post Office had other ideas, and once the canal was operating, tried to reduce the mail subsidy paid to P&O by £30,000 because it argued that costs to the company had been reduced by the benefit of the new waterway, and the contract was based on mail going overland for this section of the journey. The only way that P&O could get round the problem was by keeping strictly to the letter of its original contract, landing the mail at Alexandria or Suez and sending the ships through the canal to pick up the same mail at

---

[2] Howard, *The Story of P&O*, p.98.

the other end. This ludicrous arrangement continued for two more years before a more sensible agreement was reached.

There were however some more serious problems for British ships using the canal. The French, who had built the canal and operated it, had set up a sanitary board in Egypt that was intended, among other things, to keep the country free of cholera. The board decreed that any ship using the canal must produce certification to show that it had not called at any ports en route where there was known to be cholera. If a ship did not have the required paperwork, then it was not allowed to have any contact with the shore, and no one from the shore must go on board. The twist in the tail was that all ships were required to be under the control of a pilot in order to be allowed to proceed. The reality was that no ship coming from the east could present a clean bill of health from every eastern port, because at least some of them would have been places where cholera was known to be present. Fritz described not being able to go ashore at Haiphong because of cholera and this was not an isolated incident. Ships coming into Suez without the required certificate, most of which were British, were told that they must have a pilot but that he must not go on board! The result was that pilots went in a tug ahead of the ships and shouted instructions to the captain and crew. The canal company not only charged a very high price for this service but, not surprisingly, this cumbersome process frequently ended up with ships becoming stranded. Things got so bad that the British government became seriously concerned, and the Foreign Office ordered a second canal to be built, parallel to the first one, but strictly owned and operated as a British concern. A number of shipping companies were brought together, and a committee was formed with instructions to carry through the project, with £8,000,000 pledged by the government and an agreement with Ferdinand de Lesseps to carry out the work. It was only at this point that sense prevailed and a more workable system on the canal was introduced.

Another unforeseen side effect of the opening of the Suez Canal was the opportunity opened up for cargo ships to carry pilgrimage passengers for Mecca. When cargo ships had to go round the Cape to get to and from Britain they did not run up the Red Sea, and therefore even those with some passenger accommodation were nowhere near the pilgrims' sea route. Everything changed with the new canal, and Alfred Holt's Blue Funnel ships found themselves carrying considerable numbers of deck passengers to and from Jeddah as the nearest port for Mecca.

As Fritz neared the end of his journey, a card showing Chinese boys eating their lunch in Kowloon was sent on 10th December, when he must have been close to Hong Kong, where he arrived before the end of the month. He immediately sent a card with the message 'Arrived this morning all well. Go up to Canton on Wednesday to join the *Nanning*. Received your letter of Oct 20th all safe. Many thanks. Shall write next mail'. On 12th January the first picture of the *SS Nanning* was posted to May to give her an idea of the kind of ship which would be Fritz's home and workplace for the foreseeable future, and she was probably reassured by the apparent size and solidity of the ship.

Hong Kong, Canton and Macao Steamboat Company, Ltd.
S.S. "NANNING."

Postcard of the *SS Nanning* sent by Fritz to May in January 1905.

Fritz did his best to sound positive in what he wrote, but he knew he was facing a very uncertain future. He had arrived safely in China but he did so at a particular moment in time when China was visibly becoming a weaker force in the Far East, and changes were afoot on all sides. China's relationship with the wider world was in the melting pot, and its decline in power had triggered a fervent patriotic reaction which found expression in the Boxer Rebellion of 1901, and later in the Revolution of 1911, with a window of time in between.

China's relations with other countries had a cyclical pattern, alternating between putting out feelers followed by closing down and preserving her isolation. As early as 1405 the Emperor Yongle had sent out a number of naval expeditions, involving hundreds of ships, with the aim of extending China's control in the 'southern seas'. However, within thirty years, the navy had been disbanded and the Ming Dynasty turned decisively back in on itself, although there were some forays by Chinese traders, including a visit by 'three ships from China which anchored in Falmouth harbour in 1762 and held a regular on-board bazaar. They supplied silks, muslin, china, tea and handkerchiefs to people who travelled from twenty miles around and by the time of their departure, the ships had turned over an estimated £20,000 worth of business.'[3] From an official point of view, even if China had decided to turn its back on the world in the eighteenth and nineteenth centuries, there was little it could do about the outside world pressing its attention on China. What followed, even in those far off days, helped to set the scene which greeted Fritz at the beginning of the twentieth century.

The problem of foreign influence in China came to a head in the nineteenth century because of the rapidly rising importation of opium to satisfy a growing number of addicts. By 1820 some 2,000 tons of opium per annum was coming in, mainly carried by British ships bringing the drug from the colonies in Bengal in India. British traders needed commodities to trade for Chinese tea, silk and porcelain, because there was a trade deficit which had to be made

[3] Nicola Darling-Finan, *Images of Bygone Falmouth*, p.7.

up by the traders with gold and silver. It became convenient and highly profitable to make up the gap with opium, which began to be imported in increasing quantities, and soon the deficit was on the Chinese side and had to be made up in their silver and gold in such quantities that it led to an economic crisis. A series of Chinese emperors issued edicts banning the opium trade, and an appeal about its immorality was even sent directly to Queen Victoria, although it never reached her. None of these protests had any real effect on the traders until the formidable regional governor, Lin Zexu, was sent to enforce the ban, and proceeded to publicly destroy hundreds of tons of opium and blockade the ports through which it was coming. Opium traders in India and Canton were furious, and demanded compensation and military retaliation which resulted in the First Opium War (1840-42) when the British seized control of Canton and subsequently Shanghai. The Quing authorities sued for peace, and the resulting Treaty of Nanking transferred Hong Kong Island to the British 'in perpetuity', combined with twenty-one million ounces of silver by way of compensation. The treaty also established the opening up of five 'treaty ports' to foreign shipping as well as the right to reside in Canton, Xiamen and Fuzhou in the south.

Meanwhile, the decline of Quing fortunes triggered a rise in nostalgic and patriotic fervour, just as it did at the turn of the century, and this sowed the seeds of the thirteen-year long Taiping Rebellion (1851-64) in which anywhere between twenty and fifty million people were killed. It is a reflection of how little the West was aware of China that little is generally known about what was the bloodiest conflict in the history of the world, only superseded by the Second World War. A further twist to the story was that the beginning of the end for the Taiping forces was brought about by an army fighting for the Quing, but led for a time by General 'Chinese' Gordon, later killed at Khartoum in 1885. Although the Quing had defeated the Taipings, it had been at a terrible cost in human life and increasing Western involvement in Chinese affairs. Up to 1842, only Portuguese Macau and the port of Canton had been open to foreigners, but after the First Opium War and the cession of Hong Kong to the British, a whole series of further 'treaty ports' were opened up along the southern coast of China. It is these names which are threaded through Fritz's diaries and that form the setting in which he lived and worked. The ports mentioned in the diaries include Swatow (present day Shantou), Hainan (Qiongzhou), Samshui (Guangdong), and Wuchow (Wuzhou). It is some indication of the sheer scale of China that Wuchow, which was nearly 300 miles from the sea, should have been classed as a port, but that is exactly what it was, and still is, for a huge area of the interior.

It is tempting to assume that the opium trade was being pursued on the other side of the world without much interest or concern being expressed in England, but this was not the case, at least in Cornwall. The *Falmouth Packet* of 7th January 1893 recorded significant local concern:

> The Mayor of Falmouth, Mr T Webber, has received the following letter from Mr Cavendish Bentinck MP dated from the Union League Club, New York, December 27th 1892. "I beg to acknowledge the receipt of the resolution passed at a public meeting held in Falmouth on December 1st relative to the traffic of opium carried on by the Anglo-Indian Government, and beg to state the resolution shall have my best consideration."

It must have taken a local head of steam to convene a public meeting and pass a resolution on such an issue, even if it seems to have received a somewhat formal and uncommitted response from the MP, Cavendish Bentinck, who was a Conservative, and may have been rather less dynamic than his Liberal rival. Tuke, the painter and a committed Liberal supporter, described Bentinck in his diary as 'a thorough donkey' but with the 'enormous advantage of a very charming and *rich* American wife'.[4] Whatever Bentinck did or did not do, there was clearly public concern in Falmouth about the opium trade, as there had been concern about slavery earlier in the century. Cornwall may have been seen by some people as something

---

[4] Maria Tuke Sainsbury, *Henry Scott Tuke, p. 79.*

of a remote appendage to England, but it had an awareness of what was happening in the world at large, which seems to have been better informed than many places which were assumed to be more 'civilized', and the Cornish certainly had a strong sense of what was right and wrong. Presumably a lot of people just ignored the opium trade but it was more difficult to overlook if a person came into direct contact with it. Mary Fraser, a diplomat's wife travelling by ship from Venice to Peking in 1874, wrote that she could not help noticing the strange smell on board – 'the abominable, acrid, all-pervading smell of the opium cargo it was carrying'.[5] The opium trade continued until it was finally banned by the Chinese in 1906.

Fritz arrived in China just three years after the Boxer Rebellion, when the 'Harmony of Righteous Fists society' seized Beijing, killing 200 foreigners and thousands of Chinese Christians. The rising was finally crushed by a multi national force of 20,000 troops in September 1901, after which China was once again forced to pay a huge indemnity. All of this was happening on the other side of the world, a hundred years ago, when communications and media reporting were far slower and more sparse than they are today, and yet, people in Falmouth knew enough to raise a public protest about opium. The medium for the message was the press, and a local newspaper like the *Falmouth Packet* of the 1890s, carried far more national and international news than is carried by local or even the regional press today. The growth of local papers in the second half of the nineteenth century is a story in its own right, and plays its part in Fritz's awareness and perception of what was going on in the world at large. At the beginning of the nineteenth century, newspapers had to pay a stamp duty which made them expensive for ordinary people to buy, but in 1836 the duty was reduced from 4d to 1d and the tax on paper was also brought down. The price of the *Times* newspaper dropped from 7d to 5d and other papers followed suit, which made papers more affordable and brought about a rapid rise in the local press. The second half of the nineteenth century saw a dramatic increase in local newspapers, not least in Cornwall, with new titles established in Penzance, Liskeard,

---

[5] Katie Hickman, *Daughters of Britannia*, p.14.

Penryn, Redruth, Launceston, Bodmin, Newquay, Camborne, St Austell as well as Falmouth. The arrival of telegraphic communication was a major factor for local papers, enabling them to cover foreign news more quickly, with an overland cable link to India in 1865 and a submarine cable by 1870. Nationally the telegraph transformed the speed of news reporting, notably marked in 1844, when the birth of Queen Victoria's second son was communicated by the first press telegram sent from Windsor Castle, which enabled the *Times* to print the news in an edition which went to press forty minutes after the birth. Local papers could pick up international news with increasing speed, though the cost must have been a major overhead if the *Times* expenditure of £40,000 on telegraph communication in 1870 is anything to go by. By 1875, even the *Falmouth Packet* had a regular column entitled 'Central Press Telegrams' which carried the latest international news.

During the time of Fritz's apprenticeship at Cox's, the *Falmouth Packet* was carrying weekly reports of the Sino-Japanese War that was being fought over Korea. As he contemplated travelling to Hong Kong, Fritz would have been reading of the assassination of the pro-Japanese Korean leader, giving Japan an excuse to send a punitive expedition that quickly defeated the Chinese troops that had come at the request of the Koreans. The speed with which the Chinese army was smashed by the Japanese must have been apparent even thousands of miles away in England, and the cession of Taiwan and other territories to the Japanese underlined the reason why China was referred to as 'the sick man of Asia'. Perhaps of even more significance was the fact that under the Treaty of Shimonseki of 1895 which ended the war, Japan secured the opening of four more Chinese ports to outside trade, together with the right of the Japanese to build and operate factories in China. This was a further episode in the forced opening up of China to foreign influence, and Taiwan, the Pescadores and the Liaodong peninsula, which had been taken from China by Japan, were only restored to China again after the Second World War. Fritz had at least some understanding of all this and was well aware that foreign-owned shipping lines were vital to the development of trade. The story of the competing shipping lines is the final piece of the picture.

The early part of the present century has seen a massive growth in imports by Britain from China, but in the latter part of the nineteenth century the imports from China mainly consisted of tea and silk together with an increasing amount of merchandise in a 'chinese' style, but often based on designs from elsewhere. It is not immediately obvious what the West was exporting to the East apart from the trade in opium from the British colonies in India that, like slavery, was a well-known fact but not one that anyone wished to challenge too strongly at an official level. The reports on international trade that were presented to parliament at Westminster made it absolutely clear how economically important the opium trade was, and make disturbing reading today. Liverpool, with its tradition for international trading by sea, was the base for a number of companies that were keen to open up trade with China, and that were frequently headed by distinctive individuals who pursued their own lines of business in their own, often idiosyncratic, ways. John Swire stands out as one figure who became significant in Fritz's life because Swire's China Navigation Company (CNC) operated all along the China coast and had a share in the *SS Nanning* on the West River.

In the 1860s, when trade between Britain and China was developing fast, John Swire identified textiles as a good cargo for his outgoing ships, and he arranged agency deals with various manufacturers to carry grey shirting material, worsted and woollen goods. The cotton trade to America had been disrupted by the American Civil War so attention turned to other parts of the world, and the Far East provided a ready market, at least for a while. It was said at one time that 'if only we could persuade every person in China to lengthen his shirt tail by a foot, we could keep the mills in Lancashire working round the clock'.[6] When textiles ceased to be profitable, Swire moved into shipping railway and locomotive materials with an eye to the Chinese government's development of

[6] Studwell, *The China Dream.*

the railway system in northern China. Meanwhile the tea trade went through its ups and downs, especially when major importers like Australia steadily raised tariffs, and the competition from India and Ceylon became more intense. Colonel Younghusband did his best to introduce Indian tea to the Chinese negotiators in Tibet but met understandably with strong resistance. Australia also exported coal, flour, wool, lead and gold bullion to China that all had to be offloaded at ports such as Hong Kong and transferred to smaller ships to be taken inland. Kerosene was another major requirement up and down the West River, and Swire arranged agencies direct with oil companies to meet the demand.

Patterns of trade could change very quickly, and commodities based on grown crops like sugar and rice inevitably had a seasonal factor built in. The competition between trading companies was intense, and the more successful ones were those who were closest to the ground and took the trouble to build good relations with their Chinese contacts. The Russians were particularly good at this based on their experience in Manchuria, and despite the Russo-Japanese War which was raging at the time, Fritz still came across Russian traders travelling up and down the West River, although Russian ships and river boats had largely abandoned the southern China trade routes to assist the war effort further east. The latter half of the nineteenth century saw western steamship companies establish their supremacy in Chinese waters, and the Treaty of Nanking, which formally ended the First Opium War, recognized Hong Kong as a British colony, and the Chinese government also added Amoy, Foochow, Ningpo and Shanghai as 'treaty ports' with foreign trade rights alongside Canton. After China's humiliating defeat in the Second Opium War, the Treaty of Peking in 1860 also ceded Kowloon and recognized eleven more treaty ports, and in addition, opened the Yangtse to foreign trade and navigation. This extraordinary arrangement of treaty ports and special trading privileges enabled western steamship companies to get very firmly established.

The chief foreign rivals on the south China coast were Jardine Matheson's Indo-China Steam Navigation Company (ICSNC), John

Swire's CNC, and the Hong Kong, Canton & Macao Steamboat Company (HCMSC). The first Chinese flag steamship line was the China Merchants' Steam Navigation Company (CMSNC) which was formed at the end of 1872 and quickly grew in size and competitive strength, despite suspicion from Peking, where the scholar bureaucrats had been educated to despise trade and could not grasp the development potential of anything associated with foreigners. The formation of the company, which required ratification from the very top, demonstrated the gap in perception between those in power at the centre of the Chinese bureaucracy and those, mainly in the south-west, who had experience of western traders and were also aware that opportunities for developing home-based trading could be lost. The moving light behind the success of the CMSNC was Tong King-sing who had been a Jardine comprador in Shanghai but with shares in a joint shipping venture with his employers. Tong left Jardine's and took on the ailing CMSNC and devised a western-style joint stock company but set within a traditional Chinese structure. The clue to its cunning structure lay in the fact that although it was known in English as the China Merchants' Steam Navigation Company, its official designation was the Bureau of Merchants Invited to Operate Steamships! Tong has largely been forgotten but he was perhaps China's first modern entrepreneur.[7]

Some of the western shipping lines joined forces and shared out business in order to outmanoeuvre their rivals, particularly the CMSNC. Since trading had begun in earnest based on Hong Kong and Canton, the key players were keen to secure rights in that area and there was considerable jockeying for position. Russell & Co, an American shipping company, was persuaded to withdraw from the river routes around Canton in return for an agreement with the HCMSC not to run steamers on the Yangtse or between Shanghai and Ningpo for a twelve-year period from 1866. In 1879 Swire's CNC agreed a settlement with the HCMSC to share business on the basis of three-eighths CNC and five-eighths HCMSC. The

---

[7] For a fuller account, see *The Thistle and the Jade*.

the Pearl River Delta with its capital Guangzhou (Canton) and describes the region as 'the world's workshop' with its strategic connection with Hong Kong as a channel for foreign investment. Even Mao Tse-Tung recognized the importance of Guangzhou and earmarked it as China's principal industrial centre and international port.

The fact that Canton was a hive of activity for business and manufacturing did not detract from its more picturesque side, and Fritz sent postcards of pagodas and gardens, noting that one of the pagodas was a mosque erected by Arabian merchants who were regular visitors to Canton over a thousand years before western traders appeared on the scene. Beyond the permanent city buildings was a floating suburb which can now be seen from space on Internet websites, and has probably not changed very greatly from what Fritz saw as he sailed past it in the *Nanning*. For a distance of four miles along the river was a gently undulating mass of boats occupied by thousands of families who lived the whole of their lives on the water. Beyond the boats, moored in the middle of the river, were large Chinese junks of up to a thousand tons, which traded down the coast as far as the Straits Settlements and carried cannons for protection on their upper decks. Trade was the lifeblood of Canton and it was logical that the city had been the first to be opened to foreign merchants, added to which it was the most distant port from the capital Peking and was therefore well distanced from the Chinese government that wanted to resist any unnecessary contact with foreigners. There were strict official limitations on who might be involved in trading and only a limited number of merchants were allowed to trade with foreigners. They were usually men of considerable property and were well known for integrity in their transactions, as well as being required to guarantee the payment of customs duties. This system of authorized merchants developed into the role of the comprador, without whom foreign companies would have been unable to operate in China.

As trading between China and the outside world developed, so foreign merchants quickly discovered that they needed middlemen who would act for them in relation to their fellow

Chinese. The main disadvantage for foreign merchants was that they seldom had any real knowledge of the language, but even more importantly, they did not understand Chinese trading practices which were largely regulated by merchant guilds rather than any national or regional authorities. A merchant needed to know who he could trust and how he could get merchandise handled and moved safely, and since there was no equivalent of a police force, he also needed to be sure that he was not contravening local regulations and customs. In many ways, the foreign merchant in the China of the nineteenth century found a situation very similar that which existed in Europe some 400 years previously. The comprador, or Mai-pan (selling manager) in Chinese, had two functions. The first and most obvious was to act as the purchasing and selling agent for the foreign merchant, while the second function was to be the guarantor of good faith and financial probity of the Chinese staff who were employed in the process. When appointed, the comprador had to provide evidence in cash of his own honesty by a mortgage on his property, or via bonds from his friends, or a combination of both. In turn, those who worked for the comprador had to provide him with security, and the best security came from employing family members, with the result that staff tended to be made up of relatives, particularly in the cashier's office.

Compradors were not particularly liked by their fellow Chinese who may well have been jealous of their success or simply wanted to cause their downfall in order to take their place. In 1914 Hong Kong suffered from a spell of 'comprador trouble' with widespread rumours about the Mok family, probably triggered by the absconding of the Hong Kong and Shanghai Banking Company's comprador. The rumours were however soon disproved and it was found that the source had been a certain Ho Fook and a number of non-Chinese trying to gain control of trading in the colony. The guarantor system seems to have worked in most cases, and in 1899 when Jardine's comprador absconded with liabilities estimated at $100,000, the $26,000 that was owed to the firm was recovered from the guarantor. The comprador provided all the services needed by the foreign merchant in handling goods including safe custody, stowage and delivery. He employed currency-exchange specialists, interpreters, coolies and guardsmen, and without the comprador nothing could happen. Fritz complained more than once that the *Nanning* was prevented from sailing on time because the comprador had not turned up, and it is clear from the way that he referred to him that the comprador was not someone who could be ignored.

Since Canton was first in the field of ports open to foreign trade, most of the compradors were Cantonese, and the Canton guilds, of which the comprador would have been a member, were strong and influential. Compradors themselves might work with particular companies over several generations and they often became very wealthy and important people. In the words of a foreign news editor in China in the late nineteenth century, 'the compradore may be regarded as not only the axle on which the whole wheel of the foreigner's business with the native turns, but, in many cases, also the hub, the spokes, the rim, and, in fact, the whole wheel, save the paint, which may be taken to represent the firm which gives it the colour of its name.'[2]

Trade was secured largely by the use of force by foreign powers, often in response to resistance from the Chinese in carrying through all aspects of agreements, or at least, that is how it was usually presented in history written by western historians. Under the Nanking Treaty of 1842, four ports had been opened up to foreign trade (Shanghai, Ningpo, Fuchow and Amoy) and foreigners were granted permission to enter the city of Canton from which they had been excluded up to that point in time. However, the Chinese refused to honour this final part of the agreement with the result that there were endless disputes until war was finally declared in 1856, on the pretext of an insult offered to the British flag by the capture of some Chinese on board the *Arrow*, a small craft trading under British registration. The declaration of war and the beginning of official hostilities was of course hugely resented by the Chinese, and a mob wrecked a number of foreign factories in Canton with

[2] *The Economic Journal*, Vol 21, No 84, December 1911.

the predictable result that an armed force was sent out especially from England, under the command of Sir Charles Straubenzee, with orders to restore order. Canton was taken in 1857, and from then until 1861 the city was occupied by a British and French garrison, and administration of the city was carried out by an allied commission, consisting of two British officers and one French officer acting under the direction of a British general. Normality returned in 1861 and Canton remained open to foreigners of all nationalities from then on.

Although peace had been restored, an interesting new situation arose, because there was then a need to provide space for a settlement of foreign merchants whose factories had been destroyed by mobs. In such a crowded city, with a large part of the indigenous population being afloat on the river because of lack of space elsewhere, it was not immediately obvious what could be done. The solution lay in an extensive mudflat lying to the west of the old factory site and known, perhaps euphemistically, as Shamien, or 'The Sand Flats'. The site was converted into an artificial island by building a massive embankment of granite around it, forming a roughly oval island. Postcards sent by Fritz show the island and its stone surround, with a 100-foot wide canal on its northern side separating it from the city itself. According to a description of the time, there were two iron gates with narrow bridges, which connected the island to the main city, but the gates were closed at ten o'clock at night to keep any Chinese out. The British portion of the island was laid out in eighty-two lots which, with the prospect of growing trade, acquired a considerable sale value, particularly for those with a river frontage. Although there was an initial trade slump which hit plot values and delayed development, the construction of the British Consulate in 1865 restored confidence, and merchants were quick to secure plots and put up buildings. A ground rent was payable in cash to the Chinese government, so for once, everyone seemed to have benefited.

Shamien Island figured prominently in Fritz's diaries because it was the place in Canton to which he naturally gravitated because of its facilities for foreign crew members. In many ways the island was ideally situated for trade. It was close to the western suburb of Canton where most of the wholesale dealers, merchants and brokers had their premises, and the island also had the great advantage of facing the broad channel to the sea known as the Macau Passage, up which wafted cool breezes following the line of the river. The river adjacent to the island also offered safe anchorage for steamers of up to 1,000 tons and was ideal for the HCMSC operating its service to Wuchow. The steamer landings were only a few minutes' walk from the Victoria Hotel which was advertised as 'the only hotel in Canton', which presumably meant that it was the only place that Europeans would recognize as a hotel and was not run by natives. The hotel occupied a site near the English Bridge and the British Consulate, and could therefore be assumed to be safe. Board and residence was charged at between $6 and $8 per day, with a healthy reduction for weekly or monthly bookings. Breakfast cost 75 cents, with Tiffin at $1 and Dinner at $1.50.

Fritz would have been fascinated to see how the foreign legacy lives on into the present day. Most of Canton has been 'modernized' with brash square high-rise buildings of steel and glass, but Shamian Island, as it's called today, has remained much as it was, and is described in present-day tour guides as being the city's most picturesque area, connected to the rest of Guangzhou by several bridges, and its avenues, colonial buildings and open spaces exuding an air of brisk gentility. Shamian continues to be a thriving working community and the only reminder of more turbulent times are the antique cannons pointing out over the river. In recent years, the most significant change to the island has been the construction of the multi-storey White Swan Hotel in 1983, and it is a reflection of the change over time that many of the shops close to the hotel stock pushchairs and baby clothes to meet the demand of the many Americans who come to China to adopt babies, and who base themselves near the US Consulate at the western end of the island – an interesting variation on the theme of the occupation of Shamian by foreigners.

Once Hong Kong had become established as a British colony it became essential to have good communications by sea with

Canton, and there was frantic competition between shipping lines that each tried to gain a monopoly on the Canton – Macao – Hong Kong route, until the HCMSC agreed a deal with the CNC to divide the trade five-eighths to HCMSC and three-eighths to the CNC. This new state of affairs enabled HCMSC to modernize its fleet and to extend its services to the West River, which flowed into the Pearl River Delta and gave access to a rich agricultural hinterland stretching between two and three hundred miles inland from Canton, where the new treaty ports of Wuchow, Samshui and Kongmoon had been opened up in 1897. However, things did not work out as expected, and within a year the direct line from Hong Kong up the West River was abandoned, and some of the new smaller ships and lighters were sold off in favour of the larger sternwheelers, the *Nanning* and the *Sainam*, which proved more suitable for the river trade and which were joined by the newly completed *Tak Hing*. A further attempt to provide a direct line from Hong Kong to the West River was tried in 1904 but once again proved disappointing, with the result that the *Tak Hing* was sold, although two ships, the *Lin Tan* and the *Sanui*, were retained for a further attempt to provide a direct service.

The West River was the third largest river in the Chinese Empire, and second only to the Yangtse in importance for trade into the interior from Canton and Hong Kong. The river remained strictly closed by the Chinese government to foreign traffic until 6th June 1897 when new possibilities suddenly opened up for the steamer companies. Fritz arrived at the end of 1904 to take up his post as engineer on the river steamer *Nanning*, which was already a well-established vessel on the river, making the journey from Canton to Wuchow three times a week. The fare between Canton and Wuchow was $10 each way, and meals were served at $1.50 a time. Guides could be provided at $2 per day plus a charge for a sedan chair of $1.50, and a further $2 to cover the 'sundry small fees to be paid to priests, caretakers and others' at the temples and other sites to be visited on the route. The fare from Hong Kong to Wuchow, with a sleeping berth and all meals, was $20 single and $35 return.

The trip was delightfully described in a little guide published by the China Baptist Publication Society in 1903, written by R D Thomas, who travelled the route regularly as a guide and was the captain of the *Tak Hing* before she was withdrawn from the route. The scene that Thomas described was the one which greeted Fritz as he began his new job and set sail for the first time with the *Nanning* out of Canton, travelling south towards Hong Kong, before turning sharply west across the delta for Wuchow. The steamer could carry 10 saloon passengers who were accommodated in large and airy cabins on the upper deck, while on the lower deck there was space for 600 Chinese who were kept strictly to their own part of the vessel, and needless to say, did not have the benefit of large airy cabins. The company's handbook for passengers made quite sure that no one was left in any doubt about what was provided:

> All the larger vessels were built in Scotland of steel or iron, light draft, and especially adapted for the trade they are engaged in. Most of the native passengers are carried on the lower deck and on this deck some of the cargo also is stowed. In the after part of the upper deck is a saloon for the better class of native passengers. The Officers and Engineer are quartered amidships. The whole of the forward part of the steamer (quite isolated from the native passengers) is reserved for the first saloon passengers. European watchmen, well armed, are stationed at various parts of the vessel and all reasonable precaution is taken to ensure the safety of the steamer and the lives of those on board.[3]

When the signal was given, the sternwheeler, of about 570 tons, set off down the Front Reach passing the moored flower boats with their blackwood tables and stools inlaid with mother of pearl, and looking quite magical at night with their lamps lit and dozens of mirrors casting reflections on the water. The boats provided romantic settings in which people could meet, and it was always strongly asserted that such meetings were 'for business purposes' and the boat owners hotly denied that they were brothels.

---

[3] *HCMSC Handbook*, 1900.

The next landmark was the Roman Catholic cathedral which had been built on the site of Commissioner Yeh's Yamun, which was demolished by the victorious English and French armies when they stormed Canton in 1857 and captured the commissioner and sent him to Calcutta, where he remained as a prisoner until he died. The Chinese must have been only too aware of being on the receiving end of foreign oppression in relatively recent times, and the presence of this alien building on such a sensitive site was hugely resented, and regarded as an insult. In contrast, a little further on, a number of large square towers could be seen, which stood like a line of forts, and were described as 'pawnshops', but were in reality the banks or safe deposits of South China, where valuable commodities such as silks and furs were stored for safety. The towers had narrow slits instead of windows, and there were large jars of vitriol on the roofs which the keepers could pour down on any would-be robbers.

Around a bend or two could be seen a high smoke stack that belonged to the electric light station which supplied electricity to the foreign settlements, and also to some of the large Chinese houses in the town. Another stack, a bit further on, marked the mint that turned out silver dollars and copper cents, of which the latter were highly sought after by people living at a distance from Canton. Hardly surprisingly they did not like the ten-cent coin with the king or queen's head on it, which was referred to as the 'devil's head money'.

The ship carried on past the moored gunboats of the Canton squadron, and the Whampoa shipyards, before coming to a leper village which exacted a toll from all native craft entering Canton. The trick was to obtain a pass from the head leper which would enable the boat to pass on unmolested, otherwise any number of individual lepers could demand a fee and progress could be completely halted by a scrum of people. Beyond the leper village was moored a large fleet of fine seagoing junks, all armed with large cannon on their decks, and prepared for the run down the south coast to the salt pans, where they loaded up and sailed back to Canton to off-load onto smaller boats to take the salt inland for sale. Salt was a government monopoly to be carried only by junks and without the involvement of any native or foreign steamers because the Chinese were well aware that if anyone else became involved, then the trade would be diverted to European markets, whereas it could be sold at a very good price in inland China where it was something of a luxury, and duty was levied at every barrier through which it passed.

Alongside the channel to sea were huge fields of vegetables and fruit trees, which thrived on the fertile delta soil, and supplied Hong Kong with nearly all the fresh produce it needed, at a rate of fifty to a hundred and fifty tons per day, by steamer. Just before the vegetable area was a small temple marking the point at which foreign troops had landed in 1857 to attack the city, and it was a reminder in Chinese terms, that such a strategy had been seen as improper and unfair 'to come in backside' from a direction that was covered by only a few defending guns. Further downstream was the old treaty port of Whampoa with two very fine stone-built docks for ship repairing, protected on the seaward side by forts with quick-firing guns. The port was also marked by the 'pencil pagoda', built by a successful student, and a place to which many students went to 'chin chin' (worship) hoping for good joss for their exams. Nearby, up a side creek, was a temple dedicated to Marco Polo as the first European to come to China, and a place to which thousands came to worship on the thirteenth day of the second moon.

Leaving Whampoa, the ship passed through a very flat area of country with massive rice fields stretching for miles either side of the river, before the need to turn abruptly to the west at Forbes Point, leaving the Pearl River and entering a network of creeks to get across the delta and reach the West River. Numerous pagodas appeared on the banks as well as extensive areas of banana palms stretching out from the waterway. Among other craft on the water were huge boats with overhanging sides, which turned out to be giant floating duck farms, which could carry as many as 3,000 ducks and would move up and down the rivers, letting down bamboo ramps for the ducks to go ashore each day to forage, before being called back on board in the evening. The ducks knew the routine well and obeyed without question when they were summoned, not so much out of loyalty, but rather because they knew that any latecomers would get a thrashing.

Soon the ship began to pass through the famous silk district of Canton with the river banks covered in small, rich, green mulberry bushes rather than the trees that might have been expected. The silk farmers found that mulberry leaves to feed the silk worms were best produced on slender branches reaching to a height of about seven feet, which could then be cut to the ground in November and covered with a three-inch layer of rich river mud, ready to shoot again in the following February. The leaves were harvested and chopped up very small to feed to the worms, but fed in increasingly larger pieces as the worms grew bigger. Somewhat disconcertingly, the fields of mulberry bushes gave way to riverbanks covered in graves, laid very close together, with signs of considerable activity. The most sought-after burial place for the Chinese was on a hillside facing running water, and the banks of the river at this point provided the perfect setting, although there were some difficulties about being laid to rest in one place for ever. The local priests ran a thriving business based on persuading people that if they moved their relative's grave to a different part of the bank, then they might have better joss. Money of course changed hands for this service, and if things did not improve for the family then another move might be suggested, at a further fee.

After passing through quite flat country, the banks of the river began to rise and after Kum Chuk (Sweet Bamboo) there were rapids caused by the rising land making water drain more quickly out of the delta than the river flowed in. All native craft passing over this turbulent water made an offering to the particular devil who was supposed to live there, which meant that launches blew their whistles three times while smaller craft offered burning paper on the water. Having negotiated the rapids, the ship went past Kau Kong (Nine Streams) which was notable as a place where wealthy merchants who had made their fortunes in America and Australia came to live in houses which stretched for three or four miles along the shore. Some of the larger houses had carefully carved 'literary poles' standing outside them, which denoted the level of classical degree which had been achieved by a member of the family. The right to erect a pole belonged to men who had obtained the fourth and highest degree called, Hon Lum (Forest of Pencils).

The award was more of an office than an academic qualification, and could only be attempted by those who had passed the three lower degrees, and who then had to go to the Imperial Palace in Peking and take this final exam in the presence of the Emperor himself. Success was granted to very few, and these men were the elite who then went on to become District Rulers or were deputed to act as Chancellors or Examiners in various provinces. The poles outside their ancestral homes were evidence of their achievements, and were never renewed unless another member of the same family achieved the same high honour.

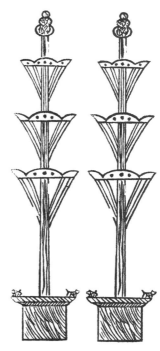

Literary poles denoting that a man had passed the highest degree, Hon Lum, (Forest of Pencils).

The exclusivity of Kau Kong was mirrored to some extent by the next settlement, Ku Lo, which was noted for its exceptionally fine tea which was exported to Europe and America and may have been the kind of tea that Fritz dispatched home soon after arriving on the river. By this time the boat was navigating part of the river which had been particularly vulnerable to flooding when the summer 'freshets' came bursting down stream, and as a means of protection, several miles of strong embankment had been built, and the local people had expressed their appreciation by sending to Fat Shan, 'The Birmingham of South China', to have two life-size buffalo calves made in cast iron. The metal animals were duly delivered, and amidst much noise and pageantry, were installed on a prominent part of the riverbank that became known at Tit Ngau Kok, Iron Buffalo Corner. As there was no further flooding on that stretch of the river, it was assumed by the local people that this was entirely due to the presence of the little buffaloes, and they were much revered. The ship continued up the river with some care and gave a wide berth to Tai Ping Chow, a large island of mud covered in sugar cane, but leaving a narrow channel through the shallows which the mud created.

Soon it was time to enter the majestic Shui Hing Gorge where the river flowed for five miles through a narrow channel bordered by almost vertical limestone cliffs rising to 2,000 feet, with a bend in the river making it appear as if the boat was entering a dark abyss with no escape. When travelling at night, the captain would call saloon passengers out of their cabins to experience the sense of sailing into a gigantic black hole until, at what seemed like the last possible moment before disaster, the ship turned and the moonlight would dimly reveal that a narrow slit of an exit was coming into sight. The gorge was a tourist attraction of the same 'karst' structure that brings thousands of people to see the same kind of scenery further up country today. The West River is famous for its passages through narrow towering gorges which have the effect of concentrating the size and force of the river after heavy rainfall. In Fritz's diary, the height of the river and the strength of the current was a constant cause for concern, and May received a number of postcards of Shui Hing, which would have done little to comfort her about his safety.

The town of Shui Hing itself was in a poor state, although its walls were well preserved and the huge iron-studded gates at the three entrances were still closed each evening at dusk. The town had seen better days when it was the provincial capital, but the arrival of foreign soldiers on the delta had caused the governor to be summoned into Canton for security, and Shui Hing never recovered its sense of importance. The hills behind the town were more widely known than the town itself because they were the only source in China of a peculiar kind of smooth, porous, black rock from which ink stones were made. Since all Chinese boys required an ink block when they started school there was huge demand for the blocks and they were sent all over the country. Measuring three inches by six, with a thickness of half an inch, the blocks had a raised rim with two depressions, one as a water reservoir, and the other larger and shallower one, for mixing the ink. The dry ink was supplied in small sticks which were broken and ground up to be mixed with water to make the quantity required at the time. The characteristic black ink was, and still is, known as 'Indian ink' when in fact it is unquestionably Chinese.

The steamer company handbook was selective in the places which it described en route and it notably did not mention Fuh-shan, which had however been remarked upon in an earlier account based on the journals of the Reverend Dr Legge, who had spent three weeks on the West River with two colleagues in 1866. The good doctor took a passionate interest in everything around him and could not help commenting on Fuh-shan, which he described as 'a most disreputable neighbourhood abounding in brothels'. Near where the doctor's boat was moored for the night were three large boats, where six or seven men 'were solacing themselves from their toils of war with certain ladies, well rouged, thrumming their guitars and screeching songs. As they kept it up well on into the night, Dr Legge and Mr Taylor paid them a visit and were courteously welcomed to tea and melons seeds.'[4] In contrast to Dr Legge, the company handbook kept to the picturesque, and described the next settlement on the journey, which was the pretty market town of Luk To (Six Knives) where one traveller in 1903 recorded his impressions:

> Here one is struck with the wonderful colouring of the hills, a very bright red, shading away to the palest pink or merging into a rich yellow, whilst the vegetation on them with its numerous shades of green makes such a picture as would be impossible to portray.[5]

Forty-five miles from the final destination of Wuchow was Tak Hing, a walled city built some 500 years previously under the

[4] Dr Legge, *Three Weeks on the West River of Canton.*
[5] R D Thomas, *A Trip on the West River*, p.31.

Emperor Hung Mo, and at this time by far the largest and most important city in this part of the province. The population had been around 25,000 but was down to about half that number when it was visited by Fritz, although the town retained its role as a trading and shipping centre for a very large inland area. Silk, rice and ground nuts formed the main local produce and there was a manufacturing industry for Chinese bed mats and bamboo hats and baskets. The *Nanning* made a regular stop at Tak Hing to off load grass for the mat makers, and take on board finished matting to go down to Canton and Hong Kong for sale. The captain of the *Tak Hing* described a stop at the town:

> Taken on board a large quantity of the most beautiful straw matting, all colours and designs that it is possible to imagine. This matting is not made here but comes from Lin Tan, a small town some twenty miles up the small river opposite the pagoda just below Tak Hing. Very little straw is grown in this district and the bulk of which this matting is made comes from Tung Kun district, up the East River, almost on the other side of the province. Large quantities of matting are also made there, but that which is made at Lin Tan is a much better quality, has a superior finish, and is known all over the world.[6]

Tak Hing contained over fifteen places of worship including a Confucian temple with an impressive entrance gate with a directive inscribed on a granite slab – 'All officials, civil and military, must get off their horses'. Just outside the town, tigers were sometimes spotted by somewhat wary inhabitants, and there was a story of a whole village setting out with guns to kill a sleeping tiger which had been spotted by children, but on reaching the spot, no one was willing to fire his gun in case he missed and the tiger attacked.

A further eighteen miles and the ship arrived at the cattle market town of Do Shing, having passed patches of sweet potatoes growing on the riverbanks in piles of river silt heaped up by local people for growing food. Then, at last, the border was reached

---

[6] R D Thomas, *A Trip on the West River*, pp.47,48.

between the province of Kwang Tung and its neighbour Kwang Si and the ship could enter Wuchow Reach, a waterway about three-quarters of a mile wide, under the lea of Wuchow Peak, standing 1,400 feet high and the place where there had been a city of refuge for women and children in the 'olden days' of the Tai Ping rebellion and other troubles. On the other side of the river, opposite Wuchow, was a pagoda 'in which a light is kept burning, during the time of the triennial examinations held in Peking, to give good joss to the students from Kwang Si'.

At Wuchow itself, 223 miles from Canton, the river was a mile and a quarter wide, with the town standing where the Fu Ho or Cassia River joined the West River on its journey to the sea. At such a strategic point there had been a settlement for thousands of years, although the buildings in the present town did not seem particularly old. However, they made up for lack of age by being notorious in other respects, and Fritz took photographs inside the temple which was designed to illustrate the torments of the ten Buddhist hells and was regarded by western visitors as something of a chamber of horrors, but one not to be missed. On a more cheerful note, 'the club' in Wuchow, where Fritz spent a considerable amount of time between sailings, was noted for having 'a first-class billiard table and everything in the way of drinks that a man could desire'. A postcard picture of Wuchow shows a rather poor and dilapidated waterfront, but part of that may be because the principal offices and shops were built on pontoons moored along the river bank, which could float up and down with the changes in river level. Even allowing for this flexibility, it is hard to imagine how a trading community worked under these conditions, and yet it is clear from the diaries that Wuchow was able to offer entertainment and hospitality and was not a bad place to be moored overnight.

It seems odd that Wuchow was designated as one of the treaty ports when the town was so far inland, but standing as it did at the limit of steamer navigation, it was certainly a very busy port through which timber, firewood, cassia, raw sugar, tobacco, hides, star aniseed, cattle and native opium were exported. Coming the other way were imports of foreign manufactured goods including shirting and kerosene, and in 1908 the value of trade passing through the maritime customs was over £1.5 million, and this was only part of the total picture. The main industries in the town were the curing and tanning of hides, the dyeing of cotton cloth, the manufacturing of old-fashioned arms, and boat building.

Wuchow had been the scene of another of Dr Legge's experiences, when he stepped ashore with a Chinese friend to distribute some religious tracts:

> He made a great mistake in not setting a price upon his pamphlets and selling them. Had he done so, he might have gone quietly through the streets, and possibly sold a good many tracts. As it was, no sooner was it known that they were given away gratis, than a crowd came on him and his followers, and compassed them about like a swarm of bees. Discriminating distribution was out of the question. Books and men were equally likely to be torn to pieces.

Dr Legge was desperate for some place of refuge and luckily happened on the Wuchow clubhouse, only to find that it was locked up, but with a ladder left helpfully outside that enabled him and his Chinese friend to scramble onto a low roof and pull the ladder up behind them. The redoubtable doctor then addressed the crowd, without much success, until he introduced his Chinese secretary Mr Tsang and asked him to say a few words. The crowd responded with some anger that a man of 'the Middle country' should believe what barbarians had to say, but fortunately came to the conclusion that it was funny, and after a hearty round of laughter, the mob melted away.

Further up the river, above Wuchow, the river threaded its way through a series of rocky defiles, forming at intervals what appeared to be inland lakes with no apparent outlets. During the summer floods the water would rise dramatically in these gorges with the result that the river at Wuchow could rise by more than sixty feet, and in 1902, the vertical rise in water level at Wuchow was measured at seventy-three feet. At first sight such a rise in water level seems unbelievable, but several times Fritz recorded a rise of five or six feet during the night while the *Nanning* was moored at Wuchow. When the weather became even wetter in mid March, Fritz noted that the water at Wuchow had risen three feet since the previous visit, and heavy rain overnight raised the river by a further six feet, so that when the *Nanning* left Wuchow, the water level was nearly nineteen feet above normal. However it was in June that heavy rain raised the river level even further, and on the 8th June, Fritz recorded the water at Wuchow at 'near the 40ft mark' and on 14th June the level was at fifty feet. Despite these huge rises in water level, the *Nanning* seems to have been able to operate a continuous service as there is no break in Fritz's record, and yet it is clear from his comments about the strong currents that it was no easy feat to navigate such a torrent. The speed and force of the river with water at anything like these levels of flood underlines the danger of navigation, and some Internet websites today have collections of riverboat photographs from this period, with a disturbing number of wrecks thrown up on the boulder-strewn shore, or wedged between jagged rocks rising out of the water close to sharp bends. It is a tribute to the *Nanning's* crew that she seems not to have got into any worse trouble than running aground occasionally, or getting snagged on steel hawsers. During this period it was probably not particularly reassuring for Fritz to receive a picture from May, which he described to his friend Mac as 'a wreck of a moonlight scene', which must have been well intended, but shows that May was perhaps not fully aware of the risks which Fritz was running on a day to day basis.

The comments in Fritz's diaries show that there was a sort of mild competition between the ships on the river, although they were working under a pooling arrangement. During his second month on the river, two American passengers travelling in the *Lin Tan* on the direct Hong Kong – Wuchow route, transferred to the *Nanning* because they were in a hurry to get to Canton, and a month later, a 'Mr, Mrs and Miss Turner' made the same arrangement, perhaps with the added attraction of being entertained with music from the phonograph in the evening as the ship sailed downstream. On 12th August the *Nanning* arrived at Wuchow in the evening but could not get alongside the 'pia' because the *Lin Tan* was already there, and in November, a month before Christmas, there seems to have been a wholesale exodus of passengers from the *Lin Tan* as 'Mrs Skelton, Mrs Jeffreys, Messrs Skelton and Purcell all came across from the *Lin Tan*' to travel on the *Nanning* down to Canton. On other occasions cargo was short because it had been picked up by other boats, and this was a sign that there was not really enough business to keep all the boats busy. Despite this competition, the relationship between the crews seems to have been cordial, as Fritz sailed his boat across to the *Lin Tan*, with Atkins a fellow crew member, before going on a shooting trip along the river near Joss House Island.

The *Nanning* and the *Sainam* worked the West River travelling in opposite directions. On Mondays, Wednesdays and Fridays one of the boats would leave Canton at 08.00, while the other would depart from Wuchow at 08.30, and they would pass each other at some point on the lower part of the river as the boat going downstream from Wuchow would be travelling considerably faster than the one going upstream from Canton. Today, the tourist focus is around Guilin to the north of Wuchow (now Wuzhou), and the river that Fritz knew so well is not an area to which tourists are taken. One of the highlights today is a fifty-mile trip down the Li River from Guilin to Yangshuo, through the heart of the now famous 'karst' landscape of near vertical cliffs and countless spires of rock, which sprout like a massive stone forest from the flat plain. This is the scenery described by the Tang Dynasty poet Han Yu as 'a blue ribbon pinned down by mountains serving as jade hairpins'. It may sound like the characteristic stuff of tourist guidebooks, but a look at an Internet satellite website gives some clue of the majestic nature of this area. The Li River landscape is now well known because of the growth in tourism and television documentary programmes looking at the geology and the wildlife, but it is not so different from further down on the West River where it is joined by the Li. This was Fritz's daily working environment and the steamer service operated, with very little interruption, through high and low water levels, and both with the current and against it.

In terms of his diary, Fritz showed much more interest in the human cargo than in what was carried in the holds or on deck. The popular perception of China in the early years of the twentieth century was still one of remoteness, harbouring both romantic and real danger. In 1846, 'the citizens of Aberdeen were electrified by the appearance of three live natives of the "Flowery Land". Strangers, eighteen years of age, dressed in blue tunics, silk shoes with wooden soles, silk caps and each with a plaited queue of hair. [They had] come from Hong Kong with Rev Dr Legge [to be] under the care of Rev Mr Hill of Huntly for religious and secular instruction.'[7] This report from Scotland was picked up by the *Falmouth Packet* , and its exotic image of 'the Chinee' reflects a widely held image. The British view of foreigners was best reflected, with all its idiosyncrasies, in the advice which was given to diplomats going out to Japan, who were warned about the danger of disaffected samurai who openly walked the streets, never without their deadly swords by their sides, and were not averse to attacking any foreigner who displeased them. Embassy staff were instructed to carry a pistol at all times, and since the samurai sword was so feared, the advice was to 'shoot to kill as soon as one saw an inch of blade'. The situation in China was much less threatening than in Japan and resentment of foreign 'barbarians' was confined to occasional shouted abuse in cities, and intense but silent curiosity in rural areas.

Against the background of what was thought to be the situation in China, it is quite surprising to find that Fritz's experience was of a wide variety of individuals of different nationalities, with both men and women travelling alone, as well as in families and groups. His diary entries are brief, but he wrote enough to give a flavour of what individual passengers were like, and what impression they made on the crew and their fellow travellers. An 'American lady and gent' were in a hurry so they transferred to the *Nanning* from the *Lin Tan* on 16th January in order to get to Canton more quickly. Two more Americans, Mr and Mrs Barrons, came on board a day later and were probably from an American Baptist mission in the area.

---

[7] *Falmouth Packet*, 16th May 1846.

Later in the year 'two Dutch Americans return with us'. Some passengers were less agreeable than others, and Fritz commented on a 'Norwegian Argentine gass bag, whom a bath would improve' who was a passenger in August. Fritz knew Norway from his early years and he either saw through what the 'gass bag' was saying, or perhaps he resented a Norwegian who so obviously did not care about personal hygiene. Perhaps he felt more at home with a 'Cornish American born at Fowey' who travelled in December. Families, and women travelling alone or with a female companion, were not uncommon. In January Mrs Faulkner and her niece Miss Kay were travelling, and on the same trip Dr and Mrs McDonald and their two children were passengers. Mr and Mrs Turner and their daughter were passengers in March, and in November the *Nanning* 'picked up a lady passenger (missionary) at Shui Hing for Canton'. Fritz was very much aware of whether there were European passengers or not, and frequently the diary entry is simply 'No Europeans'. Apart from individuals, there were some groups which were readily identifiable, such as the 'large party of bankers' who arrived in Canton in September, and missionaries were also easy to recognize, and it is not immediately clear what Fritz thought of them as regular travellers on the boat. He had been brought up with a non-conformist background and it is clear from the kind of books he was reading that he had an interest in religious matters and in the lives of men and women of faith, yet the absence of positive comment about the missionaries among the passengers tends to indicate some reservation on Fritz's part, for which there might be good reason. Missionary bodies had something of a reputation for their superior attitude towards the ordinary Chinese, and some of this may have rubbed off in the direction of crew members of the *Nanning*, despite the fact that the officers were mainly European. Fritz noted 'some missionaries with Mrs McCloy' in January, 'plenty of Alliance and Baptist Missionaries' in July, and 'several RC priests as passengers' a few days after the Baptists had been on board.

Fritz arrived in China within two years of the end of the Boxer Rebellion which was primarily a reaction against the growing influence of foreigners in China, made worse by the churlish ill manners of many foreigners, coupled with their openly expressed contempt for Chinese people and their way of life. Although this attitude was common among merchants and officials, it was, strangely enough, often at its worst among missionaries. There seemed to be an assumption among some, that what they believed to be the superiority of their faith excused offensive behaviour towards other people. An amazing example of this exclusive elitism was an instrument, negotiated in March 1899 by the French Legation with the Chinese foreign office, which conferred on French Roman Catholic bishops the precedence and privileges of Mandarins, including the coveted 'button',[8] together with armed and uniformed escorts and a one-gun salute. For people to whom 'face', ceremonial and outward appearances were all important, it is not difficult to see how much resentment would be caused. It followed that missionaries and their converts, especially those of the Roman Catholic Church, were often among the first victims of mobs during unrest.

There is less documentary evidence of what the Chinese felt about foreigners, but there is a revealing comment in the diary of Li Hung Chang, the Governor of Shanghai, recording his admiration for 'Chinese Gordon' who had come to help relieve the city from the threat of the Taipings. 'It is a direct blessing from Heaven,' he noted, 'the coming of this British Gordon... He is superior in manner and bearing to any of the foreigners whom I have come into contact with, and does not show outwardly the conceit which makes most of them repugnant in my sight.'[9] Even at an exalted level, there were attempts by Chinese to try and relate to foreigners in ways which were thought to be appropriate. In 1901, the formidable Empress Dowager Tzu Hsi received an ambassador's wife, Susan Townley, in the 'Holy of Holies' at the heart of the Forbidden City, and did her best to make her guest feel at home by providing a European dining table covered with American oil-cloth and dining chairs. The visitors were impressed by their hostess's thoughtfulness, but struck by the incongruity of rather drab western

---

[8] Mark of rank attached to a Mandarin's hat.
[9] *Lytton Strachey Eminent Victorians.*

furniture in the midst of all the oriental magnificence. It puts the question into sharp relief as to whether the ambassador's household would have given any thought to providing furniture suited to any Chinese visitors.

Fritz's own views of the Chinese emerged in some notes that he made for what was perhaps a lecture on China when he was back in England. He listed the 'natural characteristics of the Chinee' as politeness, honesty, open-handedness, flattery and curiosity. He described the way that a typical greeting by a Chinaman would eulogize the person being addressed but would belittle his own family and possessions. Honesty was a mainstay of normal business and it was said that the first things a Chinese businessman would save in a fire would be his account books, whereas in many other Eastern cultures the accounts would be happily consigned to the flames. Fritz was very much aware of the curiosity of the people he met and the questions that they asked him about his family and even his salary! He noted that they were ready to trust foreigners provided that they were treated properly by them, and in this respect he was aware of the sensitivity which was needed if a Chinese man was accused of wrong-doing or a falsehood. Great care was needed in the way in which something wrong was revealed, and required something of a circuitous route to the truth, rather than the direct accusation which would be the more usual western behaviour. It is not difficult to see how dismissive and overbearing behaviour by westerners would have been deeply resented and have produced some unexpected reactions.

A steady stream of postcards were carried across half the globe to May to let her know how things were going and what Fritz was doing. In January 1905 he sent a card with a calendar for the year ahead and a picture of a Hong Kong lighthouse, and perhaps time was very much on Fritz's mind and he hoped that the days would pass by quickly. A picture of Doshing was sent in February noting 'one of the ports on the West River at which we stop. You see all the houses are built on boats, called pias and are moored to the bank by chains'. In March one of several cards showed the Shui Hing Gorge, which Fritz describes as 'one of the narrow passes in the West River thro' which we go'. In April a card showed native boats at Wuchow, and Fritz wrote 'This part of the foreshore at Wuchow is a very familiar sight to us as it is close to where we lay…'

The diaries give a detached description of the condition of the West River, particularly after heavy rain, when the water could rise several feet in a few hours, and the current made navigation through the gorges difficult and dangerous. 'Very heavy rain today. Strong current from K to Samshui' was a typical note in the diary, and was probably a considerable understatement about what the day had actually been like. The cards, with their brief messages, may have been something of a clue to May as to the hazards faced by Fritz on a weekly basis, but most of what he wrote was factual description, and it is only with hindsight that the number of wrecks and the huge and sudden rises in water level give any clue to the real conditions which he experienced.

Most of the cards simply add detail and colour to the scene. A picture of a junk in July carried the message 'This is a picture of a junk that is known as a "squeeze boat" for when it is loaded it is very difficult to ascertain the amount of cargo'. At other times the cards carried Fritz's thoughts of home. A picture of a pagoda on the

West River Series   Photo Mee Cheung

Approaching the entrance to the Shui Hing Gorge on the West River

West River was sent in May, with the message 'Expect you are having nice weather in London just now. Hope to enjoy it again in a few years: this time last year I was homeward bound'. The card was written when Fritz had been in China for six months, and as far as he knew, there were roughly another four and half years to go, with the immediate prospect of the typhoon season in the offing. Perhaps this began to concentrate his thoughts because a card of a Buddhist Temple sent in August carried the tantalizing message 'Look out for next mail as I shall be sending you something I have long promised to'.

The process of securing an engagement ring for May was typical of the painstaking way in which Fritz went about doing things that he felt were important. On 9th March he wrote to George Eames in Sheffield, and although he makes no note in his diary about the contents of the letter, it was in fact a request to purchase a ring and send it out to him in China. George did what had been asked, and the precious parcel arrived in Canton on 19th May. Fritz then seems to have delayed before sending it on to May, and he may have thought of having it inscribed or monogrammed, as he had done to other gifts including a silver card case, which he sent to George Eames by way of thanks for his trouble. The gold ring set with five diamonds, for which Fritz had paid ten guineas,[10] was finally dispatched to May on 24th August, preceded by the card of the Temple to warn her that something special was on its way. Few engagement rings can have travelled quite so far before being presented to the beloved, but Fritz would have been satisfied that a good job had been done.

---

[10] £600 today.

Chapter 6

HONG KONG AND THE SOUTH CHINA SEA

In 1906 Fritz left the *Nanning* to become engineer on a coaster working across the South China Sea between Saigon, Hong Kong and Swatow. Swatow (now Shantou) was a port on the China coast 176 miles north-east of Hong Kong and set in the middle of a large sugar cane area from which the sugar was refined and exported in huge quantities to other parts of the world through Hong Kong. Fritz came to know Swatow as a place where almost anything could be purchased from cheap fans to tin wares and basic coarse porcelain. It was also well known for its pineapple cloth and its top-quality grass cloth made from 'Taiwan hemp', some of which Fritz bought to take home to Falmouth.

At the other end of the coaster's round trip was Saigon, which was 1,200 miles to the south-west of Swatow, situated on the southern tip of Indo-China. Fritz knew it as an elegant city with wide streets shaded by double rows of trees on both sides and a large number of beautiful gardens, which made Saigon one of the finest cities in the Far East. In contrast to other ports on the South China Sea, there was electric lighting and a safe water supply provided by a filtered reservoir. Fritz's ship would dock at the commercial port which lay to the south of Saigon at the mouth of the Chinese Arroyo River. Loading and unloading normally meant a stay of up to two weeks, so there was plenty of time for Fritz to explore the city and to enjoy what it had to offer. He went to cinematograph shows at the Philharmonic Hall, music and dancing at the Café Rotunda and saw Faust and *La Famille Pont-Biguet* at the theatre. As ports went, Saigon was not a bad place to be docked for a time, although Fritz chafed at the long delays which were involved in the loading of large quantities of rice from lighters which had brought their cargo down river from the inland rice fields.

Although he noted over thirty ships in his diaries, Fritz tantalisingly never mentioned the name of the ship on which he then served, though it would have been either a Jardine's or CNC vessel. Both companies knew his record on the West River and would have been satisfied that he could manage a job with more responsibility, though surprisingly with less pay. A number of ships operated along the China coast and beyond to Bangkok and the Straits Settlements, but comparatively few called at Saigon on a regular basis, so the possibilities are to some extent reduced. Fritz's new ship may have been the *Shansi*, which carried various cargoes, even on one occasion a large quantity of 'stinking fish', but mainly she carried rice from Saigon to Hong Kong for sale in the wider market. A pattern of working quickly became established, but life on the open sea involved much longer periods between ports of call, and ships ran a very much higher risk from the weather, which could produce anything from violent typhoons to thick fog. On the West River the *Nanning* had always been close to land, even though sandbanks and flood water could make life hazardous. By contrast the *Shansi* was out of sight of land for most of her time at sea, and the only points of contact with the shore were the lighthouses along the coast which had only recently been built by the safety-conscious British, rather than by the Chinese whose ocean-going junks had managed without them. Fritz kept a record of the lights as the ship passed, and together with his note of the nautical miles travelled, it is not difficult to see where he was on any particular day when at sea, and the beams from the lighthouses were like old friends which appeared out of the darkness to mark the progress of each voyage.

The longest trip for the *Shansi* was when she was required to go direct from Swatow to Saigon, a distance of 1,200 miles, which meant that she was out of sight of land for three days before the Varella light on the Indo-China coast reassured her that she was on course and less than half a day's sailing from the Padaran light, after which the pilot for the run into Saigon would be picked up off Cape St Vincent, sometimes accompanied by his wife. The weather could of course play havoc with the timings, but the overall pattern was the same, even if occasionally the ship had to stop and anchor in order to ride out particularly bad weather. In the South China Sea itself the main problem was wind and bad weather, but nearer to land, and especially near to Hong Kong and Swatow, the worry was being suddenly enveloped in fog, and ships relied on the fog signals from the lighthouses, which varied so as to be readily identifiable but also had a special Chinese flavour. At Breaker Point off Swatow, the lighthouse keeper was instructed to listen out for a ship's bell or steam whistle when fog was around, and if he heard them, then he had to fire two guns with an interval of ten seconds, and continue firing every ten minutes until the ship had passed. At the Waglan light near Hong Kong, two guns were fired with a fifteen second interval every twelve minutes, and the whole process was controlled and recorded in extraordinary detail by the British authorities. In 1904 the harbour master at Hong Kong was able to report that there had been fourteen hours and thirty-six minutes of fog at Waglan Island Station during the year, and the signal gun had been fired 1,194 times.[1]

As Fritz knew well, the eerie stillness of fog could be replaced with little warning by the violent turbulence of a typhoon, and in 1906 he witnessed the devastating aftermath of a particularly ferocious cyclone. In the early morning of the 18th September, a great typhoon struck Hong Kong and for two and a half hours this narrow concentrated storm wrought havoc. Fifteen Europeans,

---

[1] Hong Kong Harbour Master's Report 1904.

including the Bishop of Victoria who was on a diocesan tour of inspection, were drowned, and the loss of Chinese life was reported as over 3,000 but was thought to be actually twice that number. Fifty-nine European-built merchant vessels foundered and about 800 junks, and the same number of Chinese cargo boats went down. The 1,000-ton sloop *HMS Phoenix* was blown ashore and broken up and the French torpedo boat destroyer *Fronde* was broken in two. In Falmouth Fritz had seen the results of the great storm of 1891 which had blown for two days, but nothing prepared him for the unremitting wreckage caused in just a couple of hours by the 1906 typhoon in Hong Kong.

Compared with travelling on the West River, with the frequent stops to pick up cargo and passengers, life on the *Shansi* involved long periods with not very much to do except pass the time playing cards, with a little mild betting on the side. The favourite card games were Euchre and Hearts interspersed with Matador, which was a form of dominoes,[2] all of which appealed to Fritz's competitive nature as he carefully recorded his winnings and losses. When the ship was in port then it was usually all hands on deck getting cargo on or off, making sure that any repairs to machinery were carried out, and that there was enough coal for the boilers. 'Coolies' were brought in to do the dirty jobs such as loading coal carried in baskets on their heads, but it was still down to Fritz to 'caulk the furnace from inside' which he described as a 'warm job' while the ship was tied up at Saigon, and in Hong Kong he carried out some fairly major work, stripping down part of the engine to inspect the crank pins and bearings. During more than two years with the *Shansi*, there was only one recorded occasion when an outside fitter had to be brought in to do a repair job on the machinery, but otherwise all the repairs and maintenance were organized and overseen by Fritz, who hired in labour when he needed it including getting some 'boys' to do some of the really 'hot work re-lining the boiler'.

While the ship was in port, apart from sorting out the engines and the ship's cargo, there were opportunities to take time off and

---

[2] See Appendix 2 on Games.

enjoy a bit of company with men from other ships. The *Shansi* was regularly tied up near the *Laertes*, the *Amara* or the *Derwent* and there was an easy camaraderie between the crews that meant that the men could eat together and play cards. On Fritz's birthday, which he described as a 'quiet' day, Maddocks of the *Amara* arranged for a celebration dinner on board ship with venison and a wild pig which he had just shot. In Saigon the first and second mate of the *Brighton* called over for an evening, and 'Knox of the *Laertes*' was another visitor later in the week. If the weather was good then there were expeditions in the ship's boat up nearby creeks, and as the men always seemed to be armed to the teeth, the outings frequently resulted in shooting something for dinner in the unrestrained manner of the times. Some snipe or a few 'small cranes' were bagged without much difficulty and it was quite normal it seems to shoot at anything that moved, as when leaving Saigon and 'Ellis had a shot at a tiger in the river coming down' and hopefully missed.

Apart from the weather, Fritz's other preoccupation was with his own health because of the prevalence of disease and the constant risk of accidents, of which there were plenty on board ship, and recovery without immediate medical attention could take a very long time. When he hurt his foot after leaving Saigon in November, the wound quickly went septic and needed the attention of a doctor when the ship docked in Hong Kong a few days later, but the greater risk to life was probably from tropical diseases. The combination of heat and humidity, together with an abundant population of mosquitoes, meant that fevers were a constant worry and the diary noted times when Fritz did not go ashore because of the presence of cholera, and he was always careful to take seriously any signs that he was not well. There were a number of occasions when he suffered from attacks of fever and diarrhoea and yet there was only one occasion when he recorded sending for a doctor, when clearly things had become serious and the doctor had to be summoned two or three times. Most of the time Fritz relied, like everyone else, on his own resources and the remedies which he could buy on shore, and when things got really bad, he resorted to doses of Chlorodyne which he washed down with brandy in quite large quantities.[3]

Chlorodyne was originally a powerful concoction invented in the 1850s by Dr J Collis Browne, a British army surgeon in India, as a secret remedy for cholera. After he left the army he gave the formula to a pharmacist in London with the idea of manufacturing and marketing it as a patented medicine, which was registered and described in the British Pharmacopoeia of 1898 as a 'compound tincture of chloroform and morphine'. The label on the bottles advertised it as a remedy for coughs, bronchitis and asthma, as well as arresting diphtheria and 'acting like a charm in diarrhoea' and 'is the only specific in cholera and dysentery'. It seems to have worked for Fritz, and the combination of opium, morphine and brandy not surprisingly produced a deep sleep which did wonders for recovery from a particularly bad attack, enabling him on one occasion to recover sufficiently in time to have 'a little sheep's head for dinner'. Chlorodyne was a popular general medicine, which had been imported into Japan in the 1870s where a preparation with the same formula was produced by a senior military surgeon and distributed under the name Shinyaku, meaning 'divine or almighty medicine'. In England there were various attempts to copy the formula, and as early as 1864, the *Times* of 13th July recorded the successful prosecution of a Mr Richard Freeman who had claimed to be its inventor.

Perhaps it was as a result of his engineer's training that Fritz treated his diary as a personal log that included a record of what baths he took, as well as details of his bowel movements, or lack of them, when he was ill. Bathing was important for a healthy body in a hot, humid and dirty environment but it is not immediately obvious why the type of bath was sufficiently important to be recorded. Some baths were simply sea water, and presumably they consisted of cold water scooped out of the ocean which provided a short sharp shock, although Fritz's experience of swimming in the sea would have acclimatized him to the experience. Fritz's very best baths were in hot water and were taken in the engine room, and must have caused considerable interest among the crew although Fritz was so delighted with this arrangement that he was oblivious

---

[3] Two bottles for a bad bout in June 1907.

to anyone else's views on the matter. The habit of recording baths remained with him into later life and there must be very few honeymoons where such a precise record of bathing has been so faithfully preserved.

Danger however, was never very far away and during Fritz's first year with the *Shansi*, the Hong Kong harbour master recorded the sad story of a fire which gutted the *Hankow*, one of the West River ships, just after she had tied up at her pier. The blaze was sudden and violent and over one hundred people were killed including women and children who were passengers waiting on deck to disembark. The blame was laid at the door of a coolie, who was apparently smoking a cigarette while sitting on a pile of grass matting in the ship's hold, but fires were not uncommon, and Fritz noted a number of burnt-out hulks during his travels. A more insidious danger was from attacks by pirates, who were very active in coastal waters, and liked to pose as passengers in order to rob foreigners and then escape onto a junk which had been innocently lying astern of the victim's boat, and was brought alongside at a given signal. On the whole, passengers and crews cooperated with their attackers in order to avoid injury, but occasionally things went wrong. While Fritz was on the West River, a report of 1906 recorded that 'piracy in the waterways leading to Canton is rife, culminating in the attack on the British steamer *Sainam* of 349 tons of the Hong Kong Canton and Macao Steamship Company, on the evening of 13th July near Samshui on the West River, on her way from Canton to Wuchow'.[4] The master and several Indian watchmen were wounded and a missionary, the Revd R J MacDonald, was killed. The report concluded that the pirates had been caught and punished by the Chinese government, but the danger persisted, despite the fact that the British government commissioned thirteen specially designed gunboats for the defence of British shipping and sent them out in sections to be assembled at the naval dockyard at Hong Kong. The boats, which only drew two feet when fully loaded, were given delightfully benign names which belied their deadly purpose. Among the five which were assigned to the West River were *Robin, Sandpiper,*

---

[4] Hong Kong Harbour Master's Report 1906.

Snipe and Moorhen. Even when all these precautions had been put in place there continued to be a problem and, on 5th November 1906, the Foreign Secretary, Sir Edward Grey, confirmed in the House of Commons that 'commanding officers of HM ships in the West River area are to make periodic reports on the state of security of traffic on the waterways around Canton, and from time to time to suggest improvements to keep piracy in check, and this has now engaged the attention of the Commander in Chief'.[5] Fritz certainly experienced more than one pirate raid while he was on the *Nanning*, but his stories became so embroidered over time that it was impossible to tell fact from fiction. Given his arsenal of weapons and something of his competitive, not to say combative temperament, it seems likely that some of his accounts bore more than a grain of truth.

When the ship was at sea, entertainment was provided by not only endless games of cards but occasionally by the phonograph which was brought out for a musical evening, but was otherwise stored away for safety. In Hong Kong, the passing of time in port could be much more varied, with bars and theatres to cater for every taste, and travelling groups who put on shows. Fritz was happy to try out whatever was in town, ranging from the 'Zig Zag's Variety entertainment' to 'Pollards Lilliputians in *La Poupee*' and '*The Pirates of Savannah*' which he noted was 'not very exciting'. Otherwise it was sport, and there was nothing Fritz enjoyed more than a trip up Happy Valley to see a cricket match or to watch baseball, and then return to the Institute for dinner and billiards, with a small bet on the side.

Fritz liked the company of colleagues, and throughout his life he was seldom happier than when he was 'having a yarn' with friends. In China, he had two particular friends with whom he liked to spend time when he was in port, and it is frustrating that they are only referred to by their surnames, which makes them difficult to identify. 'McDougal' was first choice as company and he was the man with whom Fritz most often had dinner, and since it was almost

---

[5] British Parliamentary Papers 4th Series 164, p.95.

always on the *Honam*, it seems more than likely that he was an officer on the ship, and if not, then he was employed in some other capacity by the shipping company.

Hong Kong, Canton and Macao Steamboat Co., Ltd.
STEAMER "HONAM."

The Honam provided Fritz with a convenient and welcoming place to eat when in port.

When the ships were docked in Hong Kong, dinner was usually followed by billiards or whist at the Institute, and McDougal was always a willing companion on shooting trips or outings in a boat up one of the side creeks, or on walks on Shamien Island in Canton. In his first year on the river, Fritz arranged for photographs to be taken when the *Nanning* was moored in Canton, and McDougal appears as a man with a white pith helmet and a huge shaggy moustache, and less formal pictures show a smiling man who looks to have been good company. The other name that appears most often in the diaries is 'Heilsman', who appeared again when Fritz had returned to England. Heilsman bought one of Fritz's revolvers and his 'canvass boots' and he was a sufficiently trusted friend for Fritz to lend him money occasionally, which he faithfully paid back. Fritz also lent money to a man called 'Rule', and again, there was a record of repayments and the pattern was repeated later when Fritz had returned home, when he seems to have been willing to make loans to friends when needed.

A photograph taken on board the *Nanning* anchored off Shamien Island in Canton. Fritz is on the left holding a sword, McDougal in the centre and probably Heilsman on the right.

It is significant that Fritz kept a daily record of the letters and cards that he wrote home, and which were sent off in the mail at the next port at which the ship called. If Fritz did not mail the letters himself then they were entrusted to a fellow officer, or sometimes to the comprador, so that he knew they were in safe hands. On just two occasions he gave his letters to a man called Kwong Shing, who may have been the comprador as it is the only time that Fritz referred to a Chinese person by name. The diaries also recorded something of the excitement of receiving mail, which always involved several letters, and on one occasion a pile of thirty-six letters and six newspapers when the *Shansi* was docked in Hong Kong. Letters were the only way of keeping in touch with home, although the time lapse between sending and receiving lent them something of a sense of unreality, however welcome their arrival. Perhaps that was why newspapers and magazines were important in giving more of a sense of reality and permanence, and why Fritz had them bound into volumes so that he could keep them and read them afresh as the ship churned on its way. The *Windsor Magazine* was a favourite monthly that he continued to buy when he was back home, and as well as containing news it carried serials which would become complete novels in the bound copies. Fritz even had the *Weekly Telegraph* regularly bound and his cabin must have filled up quite quickly with these hefty volumes, but perhaps they helped to give a feeling of home, which was so difficult to capture in other ways.

Fritz was always ready to sell anything that had become surplus to requirements, and having disposed of two of his revolvers in the first few weeks in China, these were followed later by his 'canvass boots' and later one of his caps. A favoured way of disposing of larger things seems to have been through a raffle, and Fritz bought raffle tickets for 'Atkin's boat', 'Rule's gun' and even for some anonymous person's bed. Soon after the raffle for the boat Fritz recorded several boat trips into side creeks, and it may be that perhaps he won the boat and forgot to mention it in the diary. Apart from raffles there were lotteries organized by towns to raise funds and Fritz occasionally bought 'lottery slips' for the Canton, Hankow or Macao lotteries, although it is certain that his numbers never came up.

Because of the small size of his diaries, Fritz confined his entries to the bare facts of the day rather than giving space to his feelings, apart from giving vent to the exasperation caused by delays. If the coolies were slow in loading cargo, or the comprador had failed to turn up in time for the ship to catch the tide, then Fritz's frustration readily comes through the diary pages with extra large writing and the occasional exclamation mark. Otherwise the daily entries were a record of the weather and the events of the day, and even when he had finally decided to get engaged to May, it was only the record of posting off the registered package containing the ring that gave any hint that something momentous was taking place. By the same token there is nothing to show at what point he made the decision to return home, apart from the increasing number of descriptions at the beginning of 1908 of buying presents and exchanging currency. In February, Fritz's mind was clearly focussed on home as he bought a silver umbrella handle and hat pins for $3 and a silver brooch for $1.50. Perhaps more domestic thoughts had begun to enter his mind by March when he spent $25 on a grass cloth bedspread, two pillow cases, a table cover, two blouses, two 'doylys' and a cheese cover. The purchases were made when his ship called at Swatow, so it was the very best quality grass cloth and the total package represented £125 in today's values and involved some hard bargaining as Fritz managed to get a blouse down from $5.80 to $4 As the day of departure drew closer, Fritz realized that he needed to buy a number of smaller gifts for friends and relatives, and at the end of June he stocked up with a silver penholder, two sets of links, two hat pins, a stud and a brooch, all for $3. He also bought some cigars, but sent them on by post so that they would not be unduly delayed or have to run the risk of damp storage during the voyage.

Fritz had come to China to build up his financial base and in his final months there he gave careful attention to foreign exchange rates and the best ways of making sure that he did not lose out financially on his return to England. He seems to have had a small number of sterling five-pound notes, which presumably he kept for security, and in the early part of the year he exchanged these for Hong Kong dollars.[6] It is not clear why he did this unless the dollar was under pressure at the time, because three months later he was buying sterling back for dollars and arranging for drafts so that he had money available for the journey home. By the middle of June Fritz had given himself over to getting ready for departure, and in his spare time he sorted out and repaired his boxes ready for packing. He left Swatow for the last time on 1st June as the ship headed away at full speed on his final voyage to Saigon, battling a strong head wind, with the sky overcast and wet. Although Fritz was nursing a sore throat, it did not prevent him celebrating the Dragon Festival

---

[6] At the time £1 was worth 5 US dollars and 11½ Hong Kong dollars.

on the fifth day of the fifth moon, though a few days later he got a nasty mosquito bite on his foot, which began to make him wonder if fate was going to dog his last days after all. Perhaps to comfort himself, he settled down to a spate of postcard writing until he had a pile of cards to be mailed by the comprador once the ship had run in on a flood tide and docked in number seventeen berth in Saigon. As luck would have it, the loading and discharging of cargo took longer than usual and it was over two weeks before the ship could finally set sail for Fritz's last time out of Saigon. As the weather improved, so his spirits lifted and his diary entries for the last few days of June all ended with 'Getting ready for the Road'. At last the ship docked in Hong Kong on 26th June, and Fritz blew down the boilers and plugged a leaky condenser tube ready to sign off and hand over his responsibilities at the end of the month. The next two days were taken up with packing boxes, shifting luggage to the Institute, and booking a passage home with the Norddeutscher Lloyd (NDL) shipping line on their new passenger cargo steamer the *Kleist*, which was supposed to arrive in Hong Kong from Nagasaki on 1st July. A further frustration for Fritz was that the ship was delayed, and since it had not arrived by the evening, Fritz had a final dinner with McDougal on the *Honam*, and then booked into a hotel for his last night on land for five weeks.

The *Kleist* was a brand new ship of 9,000 tons, which had been at sea for less than a year, and was a welcome contrast to life on a coastal cargo boat in the South China Sea. The shipping company NDL was based in Bremen and advertised itself as the Imperial German Mail Line, 'subsidized by HIGM's Government with steamers plying the Nagasaki to Bremen route every fortnight, calling at thirteen ports on the way, including Hong Kong'.[7] Fritz woke early, ready to meet the *Kleist* when she docked at 07.00, and with the help of Mr Sell's car, he got his luggage on board and had time to settle into his cabin before she sailed at midday. He was glad to get away at last, and all the omens were good as the weather lifted and the persistent rain gave way to a fine sunny day. The good weather carried on for the next few days, and Fritz could relax and

---

[7] NDL advertisement.

pass the time playing whist on deck, and having hot baths whenever he felt like them. On the fourth day out, the *Kleist* reached Singapore and anchored in the harbour in the early evening, before coming alongside the quay a couple of hours later when there was a space. Fritz went ashore and wandered around the town for a while, but things soon became too noisy for his liking and he went back to the ship for the night, and was glad to have left by the following afternoon, although the weather had deteriorated and some heavy squalls caused some concern, because the ship was rather too close to the shore for comfort. The *Kleist* arrived at Penang the following evening, but was off again before midnight and continued on her way, while Fritz kept a careful note in his diary of the distances covered and the names of the passing lighthouses. It was part of his habit to write up his diary like a ship's log, and on the eleventh day out from Hong Kong he noted that 312 miles had been covered between midnight and noon that day, and there were 62 miles to go to Colombo, where he went ashore and bought some fruit. He might have explored a bit further around the harbour if he had known that the docks had just been rebuilt using Freeman Granite from Cornwall, but his mind was set on other things and although he was certainly thinking about Cornwall, it was not granite that was foremost in his thoughts.

After Colombo the sea got rougher and the ship was hit by heavy rain and strong squalls, but as the spray cascaded onto the decks above, Fritz was able to have naps below and pass the time with cards and having more baths. It was certainly not a time for spending much time outside, and it was not long before the sea claimed part of the awnings, which were washed over the side. On reaching Aden, Fritz went ashore and bought 200 cigarettes for 1s 6d, and a dozen postcards for a further 6d to fuel his regular mailing home, as well as sending news back to friends still in Hong Kong. By this time the shipping lanes had got busier, and the fast moving *Kleist* steamed past several other ships before reaching Suez and entering the canal. The temperature had begun to fall, and Port Said felt sufficiently cold for Fritz to put on his waistcoat for the first time since leaving Hong Kong, and all the deck awnings were taken down to prevent further losses. The town excelled in providing the cheapest postcards of the whole trip, and Fritz stocked up with fifteen for the princely sum of 2d.

The Mediterranean was cool but calm, and the *Kleist* called at Naples where Fritz bought twenty-five more postcards for 1s, before carrying on to Genoa, which was very hot, but which offered a welcome diversion at a cinematograph show. Then to Algiers where Fritz went ashore, little knowing that one of his sons would also arrive in this harbour in thirty-five year's time, but at the head of a Commando seaborne landing which would earn him the Military Cross. All was however peaceful on this trip and the next port of call was Gibraltar and the first inkling of much colder weather, with a thick fog setting in, and the ship slowing down as she thrust her way into a fresh head wind going into the Bay of Biscay. Fritz's homeward journey time, in a state-of-the-art modern steamer, was over ten days quicker than his passage out on the *Palawan,* so he was especially disappointed by the reduced speed now, as he seemed so close to home. As always he put his energy into practical things, and set about packing his gear and collecting a mound of washing from the laundry at a cost of three shillings, while at the same time he may well have reflected on the last time he was in the English Channel, when he was soaked by a freak wave on the very first day of his outward journey. At last, at 06.00 on 7th August, thirty-seven days after leaving Hong Kong, the *Kleist* arrived at Southampton and Fritz was able to go ashore to catch the 09.15 train for Templecombe.

PART FOUR

FALMOUTH

Chapter 7

MAY AND FRITZ

After five years of separation, May hurried by train to Templecombe to intercept Fritz's train from Southampton. She had made sure that she was not accompanied by any of her rather too interested relatives, and the arrangement to meet before reaching Midsomer Norton gave the couple a few hours together on their own before having to cope with everyone at Chilcompton who was longing to see who the vicar's daughter was going to marry. It is not difficult to imagine May's excitement as she waited on the station now that she knew Fritz was safely arrived in England, and their marriage was only a matter of weeks away. Fritz's diary entry for the day simply says 'Arrived Mid Norton about 2.40pm. Had lunch. Unpacked portmanteau and basket. Had long yarn in the sitting room this afternoon'.

Fritz was thirty-six when he came back from China, and although it had been an active and hard-working life on the South China Sea, he had always been fond of his food, and his waistcoat now struggled to disguise his slightly more than ample stomach. Standing five foot nine, and despite a slightly portly appearance, the man who had fought and won to secure the swimming championship of Cornwall at Penzance was still very evident in the man on whose arm May stepped off the train at Midsomer Norton. Above his shaggy beard and moustache, Fritz's most striking feature was a pair of very pale blue eyes, which had first stirred May's heart all those years before, when she had spotted him in the Grammar School playground in Falmouth and decided that he was the man for her.

May was three years younger than Fritz and only very slightly shorter than her fiancé, and although she was beginning to spread a little around the hips, she carried herself well. She had the clear and intelligent face of her mother, which expressed a softness but without sentiment and she had inherited the gentle Freeman warmth that had coloured her grandfather's letters to her grandmother when he was away from home. May enjoyed her food, and had developed her cooking and baking skills in the vicarage kitchen at Chilcompton, but was now more than ready to escape from her demanding father and set up house with Fritz, who was a man who appreciated the domestic things of life which made for comfort at home. After Sarah Page's death in 1904, May had been pressed to take on her mother's role in supporting and caring for her father William Page, but it was not a comfortable thing for her, and she did let slip in later life that her father 'was not a kind man'. This was a telling remark on May's lips because loyalty to her family was in her blood, and she did not easily speak ill of anyone, let alone her own father, but the distance between father and daughter is readily apparent from family photographs. William Page looks a stern and uncompromising man, who had been rather over conscious of his position as a Baptist minister in the Hammersmith community where his family was growing up. Perhaps he resented the control of his congregation, as compared with the relative freedom enjoyed by his Anglican contemporaries, who held sway in their parishes and could afford to incur at least some displeasure from their flock, as long as they did not permanently fall foul of too many wealthy patrons. Some of William's reserve no doubt came from being the eldest child in his family where things had not been easy because his father, who was an Inland Revenue tax collector, had spent some considerable time on half pay, leaving William's mother, Hannah, having to bring up the family while at the same time working as a governess. She bore William's father seven children, and being forty when the last child, Samuel, was born, she needed young William to shoulder family responsibilities that belonged rather to a parent than a child.

William was born in Southwark, but it was not long before the family moved out of London to Headcorn in Kent where he first felt that he wanted to become a minister in the Baptist Church. At the age of twenty he was accepted for training, and was sent to the Baptists' College at Holford House in Regents Park, where he joined thirty other earnest young men in their twenties who were studying for the ministry, while being looked after by eight house servants, a butler and a footman, so life was hardly spartan even if the regime was strict. As part of his training, William was sent out to preach at various London Baptist churches, and it was on a placement at Westminster that he first came across the Freeman family, who were very committed members of the Church. Visiting students were entertained to tea by the wealthier members of the congregation and it was on one such occasion that his eye was caught by Sarah, one of John Freeman's daughters. Once he had secured the post of minister at Chard in Somerset, William was in a position to make a proposal of marriage and the couple were married in the Baptist Chapel in Falmouth, where the Freeman family had by that time settled, on 6th April 1869. William and Sarah made their new home together in Chard, where May's elder brothers Frank and Cyril were born and William's younger sister Elizabeth Ann came to live as part of the family.

The Chard posting was followed by an invitation to Southsea as minister, and it was there, on the coast, that May and her brother John were added to the Page household, together with two servants to help with the extra work, since William was determined that his wife should not be put in the same position as his mother in having to cope with too much. Financial support from the Freeman's was also a help, as was the Freeman influence, and it was not long before an invitation came to return to London and become a minister in Hammersmith, where William in due course settled his family at the grand address of 48, Upper Mall. The move felt to William like an advance to better things, and he was able to augment his income by taking in two boarders, and with his new-found enthusiasm managed to father a fifth child by Sarah who, after a gap of six years, produced May's sister Doll, at the age of forty-five.

May Page with her family on a walking expedition in Wales. Her father William centre, with John to his right. Sarah Page on the left of the picture with May's sister Doll, and Cyril and Frank on either side of May.

The family now consisted of the three elder boys and the two younger girls, who became very close sisters, and who both looked towards teaching as a possible career and in any event a means of being self-sufficient if marriage failed to materialize. In the meantime William was also looking to the future, and having tired of the Baptist ministry, he decided that he would like to offer for ministry in the Church of England and had approached the Bishop of London, who agreed that he should go into training. William had turned sixty, but he threw himself into his new career, and in order to have somewhere to live during his training, he took Sarah and the two girls to live with his son Cyril, who had a house in St Mary Grove, Chiswick, where Cyril worked as an 'art decorator'. It was during this time that William also managed to run a school for girls, perhaps as an additional source of income, but requiring considerable practical support from both his daughters. The school employed a staff of six or seven teachers, and photographs show William proudly sporting academic dress, but with a rather less than enthusiastic May at his side.

May, seated on the left, distanced from her father in the middle with whom she had an uneasy relationship while he headed the Chiswick High School for Girls.

Meanwhile, the Bishop of London duly ordained William as a deacon in 1902, and then priest in the following year, while he served a curacy at St Anne's Soho, followed by two years at St Mary, Acton. It was while the family was at Chiswick that Sarah Page had become ill with what was eventually diagnosed as bowel cancer, but she managed to move with the family to 3 Derwentwater Mansions in Acton, where her condition slowly and painfully deteriorated until she finally died on 13th June 1904. Sarah's death coincided with the news that William was to be invited by the Bishop of Bath and Wells to take the living of Chilcompton in Somerset, and it was perhaps fortuitous that the sadness of Acton should be replaced so quickly by a move to the Southwest. It was certainly poignant that it was to Chilcompton, the place where the Page family had gone to recover immediately after Sarah's death, that May brought Fritz on his return from China.

Chilcompton vicarage was big enough for Fritz and May to be able to find some private space in which to sit and talk, although Fritz had already noted the things that needed attention. Top of the list was the garden, which to Fritz's mind was lacking the order which would be needed for the wedding. On his first morning he got up early and went out to survey the lawn and flower borders, and was not reassured by what he saw. William Page seems to have been a man who did not mind very much about his surroundings, and probably had got so used to the large unkempt garden that it would not have occurred to him that it might be a problem for the tidy-minded Fritz, who wanted the very best for May's big day. The following morning Fritz set about cutting the grass, but judiciously took the afternoon off to drive with May through Wells and Wookey Hole to see the caves and climb the rocks. Gardening continued for a further day until it was interrupted by the arrival of Fritz's boxes by Pickford's carrier, which were eagerly unpacked to reveal the treasure trove of gifts which he had brought home.

Time moved to a pattern at Chilcompton, and although there were opportunities to sit and chat and take walks out across the countryside, there were also certain things expected of the vicar's daughter, with people to visit in order to introduce the man whom everyone had been waiting to meet. As in most villages, the farms played an important part in the community and especially in relation to the church. Supper at the Cole's farm was followed a day or two later by a visit to Mattick's Farm for a tour of the cheese-making, before a hefty supper with the family. Next it was supper at Mr Candy's farm followed by a convivial evening, which meant that Fritz and May did not get back to the vicarage until nearly midnight, and the diary noted 'May and I very dusty'. May was good at playing her part in keeping things right with the parish, and people enjoyed inviting her for meals and to look round their farms. She was a warm and cheerful woman and conversation would have flowed and there would have been easy laughter, but May also had her own particular interests and passions, and one of these was shopping. Chilcompton provided the immediate necessities of daily living, but a trip to Bristol was altogether a different matter and filled May with an excitement and unlimited energy for exploring what the shops had to offer. Fritz was happy to be with May, but shopping was his least favourite pastime, and May needed to find some additional incentives to coax him along. On 13th August she took Fritz on the train to Bristol, with the promise of lunch at Cabot's and 'a turn on the Suspension bridge and a seat on the Downs'. The diary records that it was then 'More shopping, tea and shopping and finally caught the train by half an hour and arrived back safely, tired but happy'.

Fritz was more than content to be in Somerset with May, but his thoughts were turning to his family in Falmouth whom he had not yet been able to see, and a certain amount of frustration began to creep into his diary entries. 'Weather cloudy. Tried to play Patience', summed up what seems to have been a tiresome afternoon, and the following day he made sure that he and May were able to have a walk by themselves at Radstock, rather than follow dutifully in a line behind William Page and May's sister Doll at the local flower show. Matters improved a bit when May's Uncle Tom arrived with his daughter but then took a dive when May's cousin, Beattie Freeman, arrived from London. Beattie was the eldest daughter of John Joseph Freeman a solicitor in Shepperton, and had enjoyed May's company when they were both single women in their thirties, and was particularly interested to meet Fritz. The compliment was not returned by Fritz who did not like having his time with May constantly interrupted by Beattie trying to engage May in reminiscing about old times. Fritz referred to her as 'Cousin Gooseberry' and a particularly difficult day ended with the note 'Rather slow evening. Cousin Gooseberry'.

There was however light at the end of the tunnel. After patiently staying at Chilcompton for two and a half weeks, it was finally time to go to Falmouth and for Fritz to be reunited with his brothers and sisters. Fritz and May caught the ten o'clock train from Midsomer Norton to Bristol, and arrived at Falmouth at 18.20, in time for tea with Kate and supper with May's aunts at Wood Lane. The mood in Cornwall was quite different from the time in Somerset. In place of a sense of duty in visiting parishioners, Fritz was able to tumble into the bosom of his family and catch up on everything which had been happening while he was away, and May could enjoy the chatter of her sprightly aunts. There were all sorts of things to talk about and the days sped by with typically 'Lunch at the Freeman's, tea and supper with Kate'. Just as May had taken Fritz round to introduce him in Chilcompton, so Fritz was able to show May off in Falmouth although it was rather different to what she had been used to in Somerset. After the first round of calls to members of his family, Fritz took May to Cox's Foundry where he had served his time as an apprentice and established his reputation as an engineer. As a special treat, at least in Fritz's mind, he arranged for himself and May to have a trip on the famous tug *Victor*, which earned additional income in the summer from running excursions down the coast. The *Victors'* engineer was Frederick Martin who had been a deep-sea sailor but had retired after being shipwrecked in the South China Sea. He had overseen the building of the *Victor* at Cox's before joining the tug as engineer, and was well known to Fritz. May of course was not at home on a smelly steamboat on a heaving sea, and with some relief, they got off at the Lizard and had a fine drive back to Falmouth. In the course of a fortnight Fritz took May to see virtually everyone he knew in Cornwall. They visited Mrs Hooker and met Mr Gray in Camborne and they called on the Dunstons and the Saxons in Falmouth and all the Coxes. Fritz had a trip out on the Cox's boat, the *Rosebery*, to the Helford and round the Manacles, though this was without May, who had probably had enough of the sea for the time being after her trip on the *Victor*, and went shopping instead. One of the final places to visit was the Swanpool cemetery where Fritz's parents were buried and whose grave he would always look after, cutting the grass and planting flowers.

The time finally came to leave Falmouth and they caught an early train, accompanied by Fritz's niece Janet, and were seen off from the station by Kate and Mrs Humphreys. It was quite late when they got to Melton to be met by Mr Page, who drove them back to the vicarage to spend a happy evening opening wedding presents. Life at Chilcompton settled back into its accustomed pattern with walks in the countryside and visits to farms, although Fritz became increasingly restless at the thought of all the things that needed to be done before the wedding. He worked away at the garden and spent time in the carpenter's shop making repairs to garden benches, fences and plant supports, and summing it all up in the diary as 'Did a fairly good days work May's version'. On wet days it was less easy to sort out the garden, so their time was spent inside writing letters, or with both May and Fritz busy sewing since both of them were well practised with a needle and thread and it made for a companionable occupation.

Banns were called for the third and last time on Sunday 13th September and work on the garden intensified while relations began to arrive to stay. May did more shopping and Fritz set about colour washing the parish room. Kate and one of the aunts were already staying in the house and they were soon joined by cousins Louie Page and Marjorie, while Fritz began to pack up his belongings and May started to put things together for the honeymoon. Two days before the wedding, Fritz recorded the 'Aunts invasion', so he and May went for a walk after supper to have some time to themselves away from the vicarage which was now bursting at the seams. Their final evening at Chilcompton was spent with 'Music in the Drawing Room after supper', after which Fritz 'Went over to the Richmond's to sleep, turned in 1.10am'.

It was a short night for Fritz who was up early and called for May at 07.15 so that they could attend Holy Communion together before breakfast. It was either a mark of how far Mr Page had moved in his theology, or else it was one more thing expected of the vicarage family, that an ex-Baptist minister and two young adults who would become committed Baptist Sunday School teachers should attend early Communion on the couple's wedding day.

Maybe it was just something that they could do quietly at the beginning of a day that would otherwise be given over to noisy celebration with little time to reflect in peace. Whatever the reasons, it was the start of a good day, with the garden looking at its best and the parish room decked out and ready for the guests. At half past two the bride and groom were ready, and William Page conducted his daughter's wedding in Chilcompton Parish Church with Fritz's sister Kate McGill signing the register as a witness alongside May's sister Doll. At this most important moment in their lives they were supported by the two women who were closest to them, and whose love and friendship would remain with them for the rest of their lives. Everything went without a hitch, and the guests waved the couple off as they drove away from the vicarage to go to the station, and Fritz was able to forget about the jobs in the garden that had not been quite finished. He characteristically summed up the day in his diary – 'Arranged our presents. Lunch. Dress for church. Wedded at 2.30pm. Back to house, received visitors. Changed. Left for Bournemouth at 4.45. Arrived Parkstone 8.40. Supper in hotel. Card to Doll, then to bed'.

The next morning, when the newly-weds woke up, to Fritz's amazement, May decided to go shopping! It was the only entry with double exclamation marks in any of his diaries, but this was one of the things about May which Fritz loved, but never quite understood. She was a homely practical person just like her husband, and presented as she was in Bournemouth with a fine array of excellent shops, the obvious thing to do was to go out and make the most of the opportunity, and Fritz could comfort himself with the thought that he at least now had May all to himself for the next five weeks. It seems a surprisingly long honeymoon, but they had been apart for the best part of five years and each of them needed to adjust to a very different way of life to the ones that they had lived up to that point. Their time together was spent with endless walks in and around Bournemouth, and sometimes even Fritz was hard put to think of fresh routes for their perambulations as they 'zig-zagged around looking for new roads'. They walked in the Park most days with an easy walk on to Sandbanks and the possibility of a return across the moors, where they picked heather to send to Doll for the Chilcompton Harvest Festival. Little by little the distances extended further and it was not long before they were walking to Poole and then combining walking with trams so as to visit Lansdowne, Boscombe, Christchurch, Southbourne and Wimborne Minster to see the chain library. After a fortnight they felt ready for more adventurous entertainment, and went to a Symphony Concert at the Winter Gardens in Bournemouth and a hockey match between Poole and Salisbury which was played in the Park, but the Eisteddfod in Trinity Hall at Poole was not an overwhelming success as Fritz felt that there was 'rather too much Bazaa'. Both May and Fritz mailed off a steady stream of postcards to family and friends to let them know any news, and May worked on her cookery book to accommodate her husband's rather than her father's favourites. As time went on, their walks began to focus more on the coast, and the sea began to exercise its old magic on Fritz who noted their final expedition along the cliffs as a 'First-class outing'.

On 28th October five weeks was up and their stay in Bournemouth came to an end, but a new journey was opening up in front of them. Fritz and May had dutifully done the rounds in Somerset and Cornwall, but they had not so far met up with Charles and Walter in Sheffield, who were the brothers who were closest to Fritz and the ones to whom he wrote most frequently when he was away. According to the diary, Fritz 'ordered a bus' which left at 13.35 from Bournemouth and arrived at Chilcompton at 17.21 in time for tea and a quiet evening at the vicarage, recovering from four hours on the road. However there was no time to linger and the next morning they were off again, but this time on the train, arriving at Buxton at 16.47 to be met by Walter at the station. It had been over five years since Fritz had last seen Walter, although he had kept in touch by post and had frequently sent small gifts, especially cigars. The evening was spent catching up on old times and playing a number of games of billiards.

Fritz was back with his family once more, and the next few days were spent happily exploring the area on walks with May, and spending the evenings round the billiard table benefiting from all the practice on the tables at the Institute in Hong Kong and the Club at Wuchow. May warmed to the closeness of the Lewis family, as apart from her sister Doll, her brothers had all been some distance from Chilcompton, and John had migrated all the way to New Zealand to pursue his career as a doctor. As was his usual practice, Fritz noted in his diary where he and May walked each day, and it was at least a fresh area to discover. The week was quickly passed, and a train journey of an hour and half took them to Sheffield to be met by Charles at the station and taken to his house at 143 Abbeyfield Road, where they enjoyed an evening of Fritz re-telling stories and playing cards with his brother and George Eames. Fritz's eldest brother Joe also lived in Sheffield with his wife Fanny in Rock Street, but the difference in age meant a less close tie and the first time Fritz called at the house he found that Fanny was out. Most of the time was spent with the younger brothers and their families, and on a typical Saturday afternoon Fritz went with Charles and Walter to watch Sheffield United play Newcastle, while May took four of her nephews and nieces to the Albert Hall for the afternoon, to be met by the men when the match was over. The happy party sat down to tea, with Walter's son Leslie who was eleven, taking the lead, while his younger cousins, Eric, Jessie and Reggie, who came from Charles's family of six children, made the most of the day out with their aunt who clearly enjoyed their boisterous company.

Fritz had come back from China without knowing what his next job would be, so there was more involved in the trip to Sheffield than just catching up with the family. Charles and Walter would have loved to have had Fritz and May near them in the north, and there was a lot of discussion of the prospects and possibilities of business. Towards the end of the time in Sheffield, Fritz went with John Eames to visit his factory on Trent Street, where he was company secretary of a firm that produced bottled mineral water. Previously he had been to see something of the steel tool and cutlery business with which Charles, Walter and Joseph were all involved, and no doubt May talked to the two Annie's about what life was like in Sheffield. Fritz and May's walks became longer, as they had done in

Bournemouth, and there was plenty to sort out as they thought about what the future might hold for them .

By the end of November colder weather was beginning to set in, and at the Sheffield United versus Preston North End match on 28th November, Fritz recorded that he had worn his overcoat for the second time since being in Sheffield. It was clearly time to travel to warmer climes, and they left Sheffield on a foggy morning on the last day of November for a slow journey to Bath, with more delays because of the weather, before arriving eventually at Chilcompton in time for tea. The cold and damp had however taken their toll on Fritz who woke up the next morning with a 'rather bad cold', so that he had to 'take it easy', apart from a short walk round the garden which he did not find encouraging. Over the next few days the cold turned into a sore throat and a cough and there was no improvement in the weather outside, which meant that Fritz had to content himself with staying indoors and occupying himself with cleaning all Mr Page's clocks, which had suffered from the same lack of attention as his garden. Confinement inside however had some advantages, and the diary records a contented Sunday 'In bed all day and fire in room. May and I had comfy afternoon and evening. Weather fine. May reading'.

After all their travelling and living in other people's houses it was time to begin planning and to make preparations for where they were going to live, but rather surprisingly, the first thing that Fritz did was to 'write to Cowell about dress suit'. Perhaps it was all part of getting himself smartened up for the next stage of married life, but whatever it was, Cowell replied by return and Fritz wrote back to say that he was willing to pay between £3 10s and £4 for the suit. Having got that settled, he decided that his cough was now fully gone and he celebrated by going out with his rook rifle and having some pot shots at birds.

Any further thoughts about the future had to go on hold while preparations were made for the more immediate demands of Christmas. Presents would be needed for nephews and nieces so Fritz wrote an order to Gamages in London and sent it off with a thirteen-shilling postal order. He then set about helping May with making mincemeat before starting on a lengthy Christmas card list, sending cards off together with some 'cake for MacD and Hooker' in Hong Kong. The parcel duly arrived from Gamages, which meant that toys could be packed up and posted off, and time could then be spent on some garden tidying and putting up decorations. Fritz was getting his eye in with the rook rifle and shot two starlings, a thrush and a blackbird, which he then proceeded to pluck ready for the table. Christmas was celebrated in thick snow, but it was warm and cheery in the vicarage at Chilcompton as Fritz and May celebrated their first Christmas as husband and wife, little knowing that their next would be as father and mother.

Chapter 8

FALMOUTH HOME

Apart from his first five years, most of Fritz's life was lived in Falmouth and it was here that he felt most settled and at home. When he was far away in China, it was the thought of being home, and particularly being home with May Page as his wife in Falmouth, that kept him going. The hard work and the careful banking and investment of his money were all geared to that one aim, and although he and his family would have to go through their troubles in the years to come, most of what he recorded in his diaries was the solid day-to-day stuff of family life and his job with the waterworks. He was writing about what had become familiar to him and the people whom he had come to know. Some names come up over and over again, and it is these people who made up the familiar web of life of which Fritz was a part. May Page was always at the centre of his thoughts, but his elder sister Kate figures large as the person who cared for him through his mother's illness and early death when he was seven, and who was close to both Fritz and May when they were married. In China he wrote almost as frequently to

Kate as he did to May, and it was Kate who looked after his finances at home in Falmouth and who made sure that any family matters were attended to, and it was to Kate that Fritz posted the family Bible by registered post for safe keeping. Outside his immediate family it was the Coxes and the Freemans who figured particularly in his diaries and letters. May's aunts, Alice and Sophie Freeman, had an especially soft spot for their niece's new husband, and Fritz kept in touch with them in return. Among the Coxes it was Alf Cox who was Fritz's closest friend, and since they were the same age, they were either at school together or met through the Baptist church, and probably both.

May's aunts, Sophie and Alice Freeman. Sophie regularly corresponded with Fritz when he was away in China, and then persuaded him to become Bible-class teacher on his return home.

Perhaps Fritz had always assumed that Cornwall would naturally be where he and May would set up home, but their travels to Sheffield and their time at Chilcompton had raised other possibilities for them, though finally they had both come to the conclusion that Falmouth would be where they would settle. May was no stranger to the town, and the times that she had stayed at her grandmother's house in Wood Lane had been particularly happy, and her aunts in whom she was able to confide after her mother's death, knew that a move away from Chilcompton would be good for her. It only remained for them to find somewhere to live and for Fritz to find employment, and on both fronts they had friends and family who could help them. Fritz's father Arthur had died ten years previously, but he had always had an eye for property as he made his way from Harbour Terrace to Melvill Road and finally to an imposing house in Park Terrace. Arthur knew that his children would need places to live as they married and started families of their own, so he held on to his houses and assembled something of a small cluster around Marlborough Road and Albany Road. Due to Arthur's foresight Fritz was able to return to Falmouth at the beginning of 1909 and to set up home with May at 48 Marlborough Road, where it became increasingly obvious that May was pregnant. Their first child, Wilf, was born on 25th September of the same year, and the new baby was welcomed into the world by all the Lewis's as well as the McGills, the Coxes and the Freemans in Wood Lane. William Page was Wilf's only grandparent still living, but despite his reputation for being undemonstrative, he was glad to see May settled, even if privately he missed her support in Somerset.

Having secured a place to live, Fritz's next task was to find a job, and in this respect his friendship with Alf Cox was to play a vital and long-lasting part. Even for a member of the Cox clan, Alf had come a long way, and had followed in his father's footsteps by becoming Mayor of Falmouth in 1907 and 1908 while working as the Manager of the Falmouth and Penryn Waterworks Company. Alf was an ambitious man who had made good connections in the business world in the town, as well as developing his civic reputation with the town council in Falmouth and beyond, but even he was not able to combat the growing public anxiety and criticism of the way the waterworks was managing the town's water supply. To say that there was a conflict of interest would be putting it mildly, and the roots of the tension between the town and the waterworks went right back to the setting up of the Waterworks Company in 1847 and the unwillingness of local people, let alone the town council, to invest in the project or even to seek some kind of involvement, if only to exercise some influence on how the enterprise was to develop.

Towards the end of the nineteenth century, before Fritz arrived back in Falmouth, there was a flurry of reports about the gasworks and waterworks. Other towns around the country had seen the advantages of municipal ownership for utilities, partly from a financial point of view, but more particularly because of strategic control and security. Private water companies had no powers over the owners of private wells and therefore could not enforce standards of hygiene or require the rationing of water during shortages. A town council on the other hand, through its Urban Sanitary Authority, could bring together the issues relating to water supply and sewerage and make sure that there was a coherent scheme with public accountability, which would include a proper control over waste through leakage which private companies tended to ignore.

In 1896, the Urban Sanitary Authority of Falmouth commissioned Mr Arthur Silverthorne from London to inspect the gasworks and waterworks and provide a valuation, with a view to them being taken into municipal ownership. Mr Silverthorne was given free access and every assistance by the gas company, which was a local business, but when he approached the water company, he was informed in no uncertain terms by the manager, who was now Mr Joseph Goodenough Cox, that 'his instructions were to afford no facilities whatever'. Consequently, Mr Silverthorne's report was based entirely on his own observations, and he seems to have been an astute investigator and raised some disturbing questions about whether the Waterworks Company had in fact built a sufficiently large reservoir at Penryn, as it had been required to do under the original Act of 1847. He also questioned whether the Act had required too much in the way of compensation for local mills during droughts for the company to be able to guarantee an uninterrupted supply to the households of Penryn and Falmouth. These were topical questions because there had been exceptionally low rainfall in 1892 and 1893, and the shortage of rain in 1895 meant that the water level in the reservoir was so low in 1896 that no water could be released to the mills. Mr Silverthorne concluded that it would be to the Corporation's advantage to purchase the water and gas works, and then make a move to reduce the water requirements of the mills as 'the compensation clauses have proved unworkable'.[1] The report also noted that one advantage of public purchase would be that some company costs would be saved. In 1895 there were 'Directors fees of £110 10s and London expenses of £117 12s and 3d', which would not be required in the case of municipal ownership.

Although the town council seemed to be focussed on improving the water supply in general terms, there was an underlying anxiety that it was not too keen to air in public. The presence of typhoid in the town was quietly accepted at an annual rate of about eighteen cases a year, which had remained at that level for the previous four or five years. However in 1899, the number of cases shot up to a hundred and twenty in only nine months, with twelve deaths, and the council became very anxious to know if the water supply was to blame. A report by Professor A J Wanklyn in 1897 had reassured councillors that all was well, and that if the purity of the water was improved by filtration through sand, then 'the Falmouth water supply would take rank with the finest known waters'.[2] As the water supply had been cleared of blame for disease, the obvious next suspect was the sewage system, and a new assessment and report was requested. Mr Silverthorne was brought back once more and was able to confirm that that 'typhoid fever is endemic in Falmouth' and that 'it is evident that the significance of this has been entirely overlooked'.[3] The current theory was that typhoid was caused by sewer gas being drawn into water pipes by the vacuum created whenever the water supply was temporarily cut off. Mr Silverthorne acknowledged that this was what the medical profession thought at the time, but he put forward his own theory that the outbreak of disease in Falmouth had actually been caused by contamination of the water supply at source, where cesspits, farm

[1] Mr Silverthorne's Report, 1896, p.17.
[2] Prof. Wanklyn's Report, 1897, p.7.
[3] Mr Silverthorne's Report, 1899, p.2.

waste and the privies at Mabe School all overflowed into the reservoir catchment area. He made the further point that the water company was only empowered to fine people for pollution, whereas a municipal authority would have greater powers to protect water sources, and this of course, made an excellent argument for municipal ownership.

The town council was however constrained by the local ratepayers who had rejected the recommendation to purchase the gas and water companies in 1898. Undaunted, a further report on the water supply was commissioned in 1900 from Arthur F Phillips, an engineer based in Westminster, who produced what seems to have been the most comprehensive of all the reports. Mr Phillips' inspection was very detailed, and he confirmed all that had been said about pollution in the watershed and went on to demonstrate the lack of proper water pressure in the town's hydrants, as well as the absence of any definitive plan of where mains water pipes were laid. He also provided a detailed record of the blistering correspondence which had taken place between the Town Clerk and the water company from 1897 through to 1900, and he drew unwelcome attention to the fact that, although the water company had applied successfully to parliament for no less than four Acts, yet the town council seemed to have totally ignored the process, and made no attempts to seek better provisions for the town, in sharp contrast to the mill owners who had largely been able to protect their interests by making representations to parliament.

Since the town council failed to make any further progress in obtaining control of the gas and water supplies, it was the Waterworks Company that eventually had to respond to the recommendations of Mr Phillips' report. In addition to better filtration and the enlargement of existing storage capacity, the report recommended new and larger mains piping, and a more thorough inspection of consumer links to the mains, with the aim of drastically reducing the huge rate of leakage, with all the accompanying risks of contamination of the water. There was no alternative for the water company but to employ a qualified inspector who would be able to deal openly but firmly with business people as well as private householders. Fritz appeared on the scene at precisely the right moment.

There are no surviving diaries for the period from 1908 to 1915, apart from a very neat red-covered volume for 1913 which hardly contains a single word, for reasons which will become painfully clear in due course. It is inconceivable that Fritz failed to keep his own financial records during this period, and there was one battered notebook which contained figures for 1911 and 1914, but not on the consistent pattern which he had followed in previous years, and which he took up again later as if nothing had happened. The first few years back in Falmouth must have been blissful, with a young wife and family and a new home and job, and perhaps Fritz was so absorbed in his new life that he did not bother to keep a daily record. The invention and ready availability of the camera did however mean that a photographic record began to augment the written word, and the pictures of May and Wilf from this period show a happy mother, with a son who was basking in his parents' unstinting approval.

Wilf with May and Fritz at 48
Marlborough Road, Falmouth.

Life at Marlborough Road was secure, with May's aunts less than a ten-minute walk away in one direction, and other members of the Lewis family only just round the corner in Albany Road. Fritz was more than content to be a husband and father and to develop his interests in the garden and on the water, with a boat for sailing and fishing, and an allotment for producing vegetables. A proposal for providing 'cottage allotment gardens' had been included, oddly enough, in Robert Rawlinson's report of 1854.[4] Examples were cited in Birmingham and Alnwick that showed the benefits that could be obtained from such a scheme, and in the words of the report, 'To those of sedentary employments spade husbandry affords the best form of out-of-door exercise. Idle companions are shunned and the beer house is forsaken'. In China, Fritz had not been able to use the gardening skills which he had learned in Norway on the family smallholding, but once he was settled in Falmouth, he could make the most of his allotment, as well as keeping hens in the back garden at Marlborough Road. His salary from the waterworks was not as much as he had been earning as a ship's engineer, and it was also paid quarterly in arrears rather than monthly, which left prolonged periods without income which were a worry for a man who was temperamentally against debt, even if borrowing had been an option. As usual, Fritz looked for a practical solution, and made the most from his assets by selling potatoes from the allotment and eggs and chickens from his back garden, and once again keeping a careful record in a notebook. The figures look deceptively small by the standards of today, but the sale of eggs and dressed birds was bringing in between £300 and £400 a year in today's values, and potatoes were adding the equivalent of a further £100.

A daily routine became established, with Fritz setting off each day on his bicycle to inspect the reservoirs and deal with leakages and any of the other problems that arose at the waterworks, and coming home for lunch before doing his afternoon rounds. On the way back home at teatime, he usually dropped in at the allotment for vegetables, and might spend the evening plucking birds or gutting fish, or if it was the right time of year, he would be making jam. At

---

[4] Robert Rawlinson, Report to the General Board of Health, 1854.

the weekends it might be time to sort out the boats and get them ready for the water, or go fishing, or take the family out for a sail and a picnic, and possibly a bathe. Since Wilf was growing up fast, there was naturally the question about a further addition to the family, and somewhat to May's alarm, after the relatively easy arrival of Wilf, she had a series of miscarriages which undermined her confidence and made the prospect of any new pregnancy a cause of acute anxiety. She relied heavily on friends and family, and the Coxes in particular, having children of the same age, were able to give her a break by having Wilf to tea and enabling Fritz and May to have some space and time to themselves to recover from repeated disappointment.

In the spring of 1912, May found that she was pregnant once again, and an anxious nine months followed until Roderick Hubert Fritz arrived on 14th November, in good time for a special Christmas celebration. All seemed well, and the photographs of Hubert show a cheery little baby who was crawling around the back garden and smiling happily at the camera. It was never known quite what happened then, but the story that was passed down within the family was that a girl who had taken Hubert out in the pram suddenly arrived home, totally distraught, and Hubert was found to have died. It was always assumed to have been a cot death, although that would have been unusual for a baby as old as Hubert, and the death certificate noted that he had anaemia. Whatever the cause, Hubert was pronounced dead on 18th August. May was completely devastated, and Fritz was at a loss to know how to comfort her as he too tried to come to terms with what had happened. Hubert's sudden death, when he was thought to be asleep in his pram, had taken everyone completely by surprise, and the feeling that somehow more could have been done to save him was something which never completely left his parents. A sad little funeral took place, and Hubert was buried in Swanpool cemetery, in a double plot which Fritz bought specially so that he and May could one day be reunited with their baby boy.

Fritz paid 2s a month for the space in the cemetery, and throughout his life he looked after the grave, and carefully cut the

Wilf with baby Hubert who died
in 1913 aged nine months.

grass, and planted fresh flowers every spring along its rough granite kerbstones. Strangely it seems that there was never a headstone, and perhaps it was just too painful to contemplate having Hubert's name cut in granite, and setting in stone the fact that he was physically no more. The memory of Hubert never dimmed, and there was probably not a day in the rest of her life that May did not remember him and say a prayer. She carried a lock of his hair in a brooch which she always wore, and when her first grandson was born, Hubert was one of the names he was given, and she liked to remind him of why he bore the name, but the look in her eyes said more than she could ever say in words about the pain in her heart.

1913 had indeed been an *annus horribilis* for May and Fritz and it took some time for them to begin to recover and get back to any sort of normality. Fritz was fortunate in having an absorbing job which took him out of the house every day, and brought him into contact with an interesting variety of people around Falmouth, but it was much less easy for May, who was at home in Marlborough Road, the scene of their recent tragedy. During this time they relied on Wilf as a constant source of reassurance, and although he enjoyed being the centre of everyone's attention, it sometimes became a bit too much for him, and later in adult life he recalled, with a certain amount of embarrassment, the way in which he had dismissed his great-aunts, once they had delivered their presents on his birthday. He enjoyed their devotion but he could not bear being the object of what he saw as doting old ladies, and the irritation which it caused was carried with him into adult life.

Wilf on the front doorstep at Brook
Villa, 17 Trelawney Road, Falmouth.

Just as Arthur had been faced with moving his family out of Harbour Terrace with all its associations with Ellen's last days, so Fritz now realized that he needed to find a new home for May, where there would be a better chance of moving on and starting afresh. It was an uneasy time for other reasons too, as tensions were growing in Europe with the increasing likelihood of England being drawn into an armed conflict across the Channel. Life in Falmouth however, continued for most people in the normal events of ordinary lives, despite the fact that the most destructive war in history up to that point was about to be waged across the world. It may have been that very threat that made the ordinariness of daily life so important, and the worst fears for the future could be blotted out for a time in the hope that sanity and normality would return before too long. It was as if there were two worlds, and somehow they needed to be kept apart. On the one hand, there were military maps which marked the beaches near Falmouth and up the Helford, which were at risk of being used by the enemy for seaborne landings, with lines drawn to show how the six-inch coastal guns at St Anthony Head and Pendennis would be defended if the worst happened. At the same time as these defence plans were being circulated in the utmost secrecy, a brochure for the Cornish Riviera was published, including a description of Falmouth and its surroundings, in what was described by its author, Edwin T Olver, as *A Pictorial Guide and Social Souvenir for 1914-15*. The guide highlighted the advantages of Falmouth as a 'Health and Pleasure Resort' and an antidote to what was described as 'the greater physical and mental strain attendant on the turmoil and worry of life in modern days'.

As it happened, the outbreak of war came first, and the move to a new home at Brook Villa on Trelawney Road followed in 1915. For the most part, people tried to live their lives as normally as wartime would allow, and Fritz's diaries generally keep the two worlds separate, although occasionally one world intruded on the other. While he was painting his boat's sails with red paint and paraffin, there was 'bad news of naval disaster off Jutland', and a few days later he noted a 'new Bristol airship' flying overhead. There was a 'Munitions Holiday' on 28th September, and in November and December, a series of soldiers came to speak to the congregation during Sunday worship at the Baptist Chapel, and on Christmas Day, Privates Bromley, Thomson and Moorish came to tea and spent the evening with the family playing games. Gradually the impact of what was happening abroad was making itself felt at home, and the *Falmouth Packet* was by this time carrying its regular pages of 'News from the Front' with photographs of local young men who had been killed, but it was not until a member of the family died at the front, that the true horror of the war was brought home.

It was a sad but extraordinary coincidence that Fritz's nephew Lewis McGill, and Harold Cox's son Cecil, were both killed on the same day during the same engagement during the Second Battle of Ypres. It is even sadder that the news of their deaths took so long to filter back to their anxious parents. The *Falmouth Packet* of 18th June 1915 recorded the fact that 'Mr Lewis McGill, only son of J M McGill, formerly of Falmouth, went to the Front with the Canadians and is reported as missing'. Lewis McGill had linked up with his friends the Freeman brothers, who had left Falmouth and gone to Canada where he joined up with them in the 16th Battalion of the Manitoba Regiment in the Canadian Infantry. The battalion was sent to France and was involved in the Second Battle of Ypres in 1915.

The Ypres Salient was formed during the First Battle of Ypres in October and November 1914, when the British Expeditionary Force succeeded in securing the town before the onset of winter, pushing the German forces back to the Passchendale Ridge. The Second Battle of Ypres began in April 1915 and is notorious for being the first time that poisoned gas was used on the Western Front,[5] when the Germans released it into the Allied lines north of the town, where French Territorials and Algerian Colonial troops were holding the front. No one had seen a gas attack before, and the first inkling the soldiers had that there was something wrong was just after dawn, when they saw Belgian hares scampering across no-man's-land to escape a low grey cloud which was rolling slowly after them close to the ground. It did not take long for the men to realize what was happening, and since they had no gas masks or any other protective equipment, they broke and ran, leaving a four-mile gap

[5] Gas was first used in the First World War on the Eastern Front at the Battle of Bolimov.

in the front line. Fortunately the Germans were slow to grasp what had happened, and the delay gave enough time for the Canadian 1st Division to be rushed into position and improvise a new forward defence line and even launch a counter-attack, but being caught in the open, suffered heavy casualties. Soldiers' diaries record the horror of the gas attack and the fury which it caused. The Second Battle of Ypres was described by one writer as 'particularly brutal and savage, fought in anger and without compassion or quarter'.[6] Another writer said 'Second Ypres was, for its size, one of the most murderous battles of the war'.

There was little further significant activity on this front until 1917, but the April offensive claimed a huge number of lives, most of which are commemorated on one of four memorials in the area. Lewis McGill with the Canadians, and Cecil Blatch Cox who was serving with the Duke of Cornwall's Light Infantry, are both recorded on the Ypres Menin Gate Memorial, where each night, the traffic is stopped for a time and the local fire brigade sounds the last post in the roadway under the memorial's arches. In a twenty-first-century world, in which military casualties overseas are reported back by the mass media within hours, it is hard to imagine the anguish of parents and friends who must have been aware that communication with a family member had been lost, but their fate was still unknown for weeks or months. Lewis McGill was killed on 23rd April 1915, but news that he was missing did not reach the *Falmouth Packet* until the issue of 18th June, some two months later, and it is not clear when Lewis's death was finally confirmed.

While Fritz was in China, two of his nieces sent him a postcard of Swanpool to remind him of days when he had joined in sailing Lewis's model boat on the boating lake. On rising ground in the cemetery above Swanpool, Lewis McGill is commemorated on his mother Kate's headstone. The loss of Hubert in 1913, and then Lewis and Cecil in 1915, were part of a period in Fritz's life when he and May were overwhelmingly conscious of the fragility of life

---

[6] *Malcolm Brown, Imperial War Museum Book of the Western Front.*

and the deep pain of loss, and it is not really surprising that Fritz stopped writing up his diary during this period.

By 1916 Fritz was once again keeping his diary, although he may have done so before that date, and the diaries have simply disappeared. The handwriting is in ink, and there is a neatness and confidence once more as the events of each day are noted. He started the year by buying more shares in the Wampoa Dock Company in China, and at work he was fully occupied with a spate of new pipe laying to improve the water supply in Penryn. On his birthday, Fritz planted a new rhododendron given to him by May's aunts, and in March he bought himself a new Burberry mackintosh. The Waterworks Company found a new office in April, and during a family visit, Fritz persuaded Charles to help him shift the office furniture into the new premises at the Savings Bank. In May, his attention was focussed on his garden, and to combat the problem of saving his precious seedlings from predators, he got up at 06.15 one morning to go 'slugging', and much to his satisfaction, managed a haul of no less than 400 slugs. Despite the war, or perhaps because of it, May continued to hope for another child, and in 1916 she was pregnant once again and hopeful that the sadness of the previous year could be put behind them. It was however not to be, and in June a stillbirth was recorded, and once again there was the need to recover and get going again, and hope that things would work out for the better. Apart from his job, Fritz put his energies into sailing and jam making, producing nineteen pounds of gooseberry jam and twenty-eight and a half pounds of blackberry and apple in the early autumn. He also began to be involved in teaching in Sunday School, which seems to have caused him more than a little anxiety. In later years he took teaching in his stride, but at this stage of his life, he was happier with the company of men on a ship or in a pipe-laying gang, rather than the more refined atmosphere of a Baptist Bible Class. In July he worked away with May at preparing his first lesson, but 'at class did not make much of a job of it'. Fritz was used to telling workmen what to do, but it seems that the prospect of interesting an adult class in Bible stories was something which challenged his confidence, and he would probably have avoided getting involved at all if it had not been for May's aunt Sophie, who was especially fond of Fritz, and who was well remembered in Falmouth Baptist circles as the leader of the Men's Bible Class with a membership of over 100. Sophie was described as 'small in stature, but great in soul',[7] and since she was so diligent at keeping in contact with her class members when they went overseas, there were dozens of tributes from miners and quarrymen from abroad who wrote appreciatively of their correspondence with this extraordinary lady. Fritz and Sophie kept up a steady correspondence while he was in China, and photographs of the lady 'small in stature' show an interested and kindly face.

'The aunts', as Wilf called them, lived only a few minutes' walk away and had plenty of time on their hands to ponder on what May and Fritz were doing, and certainly had their own opinions to offer, especially when it came to Wilf's education. Fritz had attended the Grammar School at the bottom of Trelawney Road, and the National School was only a short distance away in the opposite direction where Marlborough Road met Clare and Woodhouse Terraces. Wilf however, was destined for Selwood House on Melvill Road, which was a private school with a playground and garden reaching down towards Avenue Road. The house is there today although the garden was built over some time ago. For some unknown reason Selwood House was always known to the boys as 'Fuzzy's', and was presided over by Mr Frank Ashby who had gained a good reputation as senior master at the Grammar School. The school has been described by another pupil [8] who was there at the same time as Wilf, as a happy and efficient place, and a school photograph of the time has a relaxed atmosphere. Mr Ashby had a good reputation in the town and the *Falmouth Packet* always covered sports days and prize-givings in detail.

Away from the waterworks, it was maritime dramas and the ever-changing sea which was the stuff of life to Fritz, and he was beside himself with excitement when he became a witness to what

[7] L A Fereday, *The Story of Falmouth Baptists*.

[8] Douglas R R Robinson, *Bar Pool*.

Selwood House School, Summer Term 1920. Headmaster Mr Frank Ashby is
seated centre, with Wilf third person on his left, arms folded.

must have been one of the first, if not *the* first, oil tanker disaster at
sea. On the 3rd November 1916, the British oil tank steamer *Ponus*
was blown ashore in a gale and struck the rocks on the southern end
of Gyllyngvase Beach at Falmouth, where she later caught fire and
burnt for two or three days. As soon as he heard about it, Fritz went
to see what had happened, and more than once in the next couple
of days, he persuaded May to go and see it too and to take Wilf with
her. It was such a dramatic event that it brought a *Times* reporter
down from London to write an account of what had happened,
although the *Falmouth Packet* of 10th November 1916 carried the full
story in detail. Bystanders watched as the stricken ship was battered
by heavy seas, but managed to launch two boats, though one
capsized almost immediately, trapping a number of men underneath
it. The ship was so close to the shore that people quickly gathered
on the beach and gave what help they could. Some men waded out
to help those in the boats, and it was reported that the second
engineer from the tanker 'jumped straight into the arms of a Mr J

B Vos 'who was one of the people on the shore'. Meanwhile the Falmouth lifeboat *Bob Newbon* was launched, but the lifeboatmen could not make headway rowing against the huge seas. A second, and more successful attempt was made with the lifeboat being towed by the tug *Victor,* and all the tanker's crew were safely rescued, apart from the second mate who insisted on staying on board.

It was about 05.30 on the morning of 4th November, when there was a loud explosion and the tanker caught fire, with clouds of smoke billowing over the shore, and the funnel was seen to topple over the side. Burning oil spread out across the bay and there was one continuous sheet of flames moving the length of the beach towards the Falmouth Hotel. Meanwhile there was concern about the fate of the second mate who was still on board, and a Lieutenant H Badger RE, who happened to be on the beach, took things into his own hands and rowed out in a dinghy with another volunteer whom he had persuaded to help him. The ship's mate had jumped into the water and was clutching a piece of wooden grating to keep himself afloat, while Lieutenant Badger found to his horror, that the dinghy which he had commandeered had a hole in it and was slowly sinking. Since it was not possible to get the man into the boat, the resourceful Lieutenant tied him to the stern and managed to pull him to the shore.

The clouds of dense black smoke continued through Saturday until the fire slowly burnt itself out on Sunday, but the smoke continued to blow inland and the beach was covered with great lumps of solidified oil. The whole event attracted crowds of people, and the *Times* reporter waxed lyrical about the spectacle of the flames dancing on the water of the bay, especially at night. Fritz made no fewer than four entries in his diary over this November weekend, and having gone down to see the wreck himself a couple of times, he dispatched May and Wilf once again to see the drama for themselves on Sunday.

A postscript to the story is provided by two illustrations which are the property of the Falmouth Art Gallery. The first is a coloured etching by Claude Hamilton Rowbotham, which is a dramatic night scene showing the tanker on fire, with shadowy figures lining the shore to watch. The etching was produced by a process known only to Rowbotham, which involved coloured inks being laid on the plate and printed direct onto the paper, rather than the more usual method of adding colour after printing. The secret of the process unfortunately went with Rowbotham to his grave. The second picture is of the lifeboat *Bob Newbon* attending another wreck, immortalised in a painting by Charles Napier Hemy entitled *Got 'em all*, which now hangs in the entrance hallway of the Falmouth Library. It was later copied in an etching by Charles O Murray, who softened the realism of Hemy's desperate survivors into something more heroic, even replacing a child being sick over the side of the lifeboat with a cheery-looking dog!

Apart from the war and the dramas in the harbour, life continued in Falmouth in its own familiar way, as Fritz settled the family into 17 Trelawney Road, which was just round the corner and down the hill from Marlborough Road. The new family home, named Brook Villa, was a solid four-square house on two floors, with a light and airy attic, surrounded on two sides by garden with views looking north towards Penryn. The back garden was bigger than the one at Marlborough Road, and Fritz soon constructed a greenhouse and chicken run, while May set to work on distempering the kitchen and employing 'a girl' at 5s 6d a week. By this time Wilf had started school, for which Fritz was paying a fee of £1 3s 6d per term, and he had established a 'dress allowance' for May of £4 10s a month. Fritz was more than happy to go shopping, and food bills show up in his accounts as 'chow', from his days in China, but May's dress allowance was presumably to cover most of the food, as well as the general household running costs apart from 'the girl'. Most of Fritz's income was spent on the home and family and include the inevitable odds and ends of life, such as a new sash cord at 10d, hobnails at 4d, cream at 5d, boracic acid at 2d and elastic for garters at 3½d, as well as the regular 2s a month for Hubert's grave and 5s for the gas account. Fritz's accounts for 1916 include his payment of the annual Rector's Rate of 9s 9d, which was still being levied under the 1664 Act of Charles II which made Falmouth a separate parish and ordered that 'a rate of sixteen pence in the pound on annual rent, should be assessed by the Mayor and Aldermen, on the owners of all houses in the town and precincts, to be paid to the parson'. This tax was greatly resented in Falmouth where a sizeable proportion of the population was not enamoured of the Established Church, but the levy continued until 1936 when it was suspended under an arrangement which gave the Rector a fixed stipend from the Rate.

Fritz's earnings from the waterworks were considerably augmented by the stocks and shares portfolio which he had patiently built up over the years. He had bought shares in the Whampoa Docks and a tea supply company while he was in China and he had money invested with the Hong Kong and Shanghai Bank, as well as with companies at home in England, with investments in the department stores, D H Evans and Selfridges, and shares in some of the Sheffield steel companies, in addition to gas companies and railways. By 1928 Fritz was receiving well over £250 per annum in dividends, which would be worth something in the region of £9,000 today, and represented about forty per cent of his total annual income. In the light of what he managed to achieve in his life, particularly in paying for his children's higher education, Fritz's financial planning was astute by any standards. His father had also been good with money, although his final estate was not large, especially after it had been shared between his seven sons and two daughters, so Fritz did not have the advantage of a large inheritance. He had always known that he would have to provide his own financial security, including an income in his old age when he could no longer go out to work. He was a lifelong member of the Freemasons, which, like many other men, he regarded as providing some measure of insurance for his family if anything should happen to him, because he knew that there was very little in the way of any other safety nets, and his job as a waterworks inspector meant that he knew only too well what the inside of the workhouse was like.

The new house provided ample room for the family, and Fritz was able to store his potatoes and chicken food in the attic, and to join May in the kitchen making jam and chutney and Christmas puddings. The allotment provided a plentiful supply of fresh vegetables, and whenever Fritz was out in the boat he fished for mackerel, or took the boys shrimping or crabbing. Shrimping was a particular favourite, and the best place for it was among the inshore seaweed on the beach at Mylor on the point opposite St Just. Fritz would roll up his trouser legs and wade about, pushing the shrimping net under the seaweed and then lifting it up and picking through the catch, throwing out debris but carefully transferring the shrimps into a rusty old tin, which he would have picked up on the beach. At last, when he was satisfied that he had enough, after emptying the tin several times into a biscuit box on the shore, he would get the boys to collect driftwood from the mass of floating debris from the docks that washed up on the beach, and he would make a fire and cook the shrimps in any old container that came to hand, and the family would feast on the freshest meal that it was possible to have. In later years, Wilf would return to the same beach at Mylor and repeat the whole thing with his own children, before the days when picking up old tins and cooking on the beach were frowned upon.

Fishing in the harbour and out into the bay brought its own rewards, with lines trailed over the side of the boat and everyone waiting for the quick jerk which meant that a mackerel or a pollack had taken the bait, which was usually a sliver of silvery skin cut from just above a mackerel's tail. In the harbour fishing was less predictable, although sometimes there could be a surprise. Fritz was particularly delighted when he persuaded Doll to put out a line and allow an unusual fish to nibble for a while on the bait before he told her to haul in what he called a 'gerrick', which was a long tube-like fish, now known as a garfish, but called several names in its time, including 'long nose' and 'sea needle', because of its shape. The gerrick was peculiar in that it had strangely green bones, which made it an unappetizing dish for the uninitiated who tended to assume that there was something wrong with it. Fritz was an experienced seaman but, like anyone else, he could be caught out when the weather changed without warning. There were occasions when he misjudged the strength of the wind, and family and friends on board had to be organized into a rowing rota in order to get the boat home. On one outing, he got it so badly wrong that he had to run into St Just and take lodgings for the night with a Mrs Pascoe and her daughter, until the wind had dropped enough for him to get up at five in the morning and struggle back to Falmouth, part sailing and part rowing. In contrast to the way in which the harbour provided a haven for shipping it could also become a container for a localized storm. Wilf's lifelong horror of lightning stemmed from being caught out in a boat in the harbour during a particularly violent storm, when lightning was striking into the sea as thunder crashed and banged immediately overhead.

Most family outings were relaxed and peaceful although they could be suddenly enlivened by Fritz's slightly offbeat sense of humour. Seagulls were a particular source of irritation, and he disliked them for the mess they made on his boats and their noisy attention on what should have been quiet fishing trips. During family picnics on the cliffs above Kynance Cove, the gulls would gather and squawk for food which Fritz obligingly provided in the form of specially made mustard sandwiches. The greedy birds gulped down the chunky offerings and took off from the cliff edge, only to be violently sick into the sea. The spectacle was not one that May encouraged, but Fritz would be beside himself with delight and the boys joined in until brought to order by May. The boys had no doubts about the fact that the bond between May and Fritz was very strong, but they were sometimes afraid that Fritz might just push things a bit too far. May was, after all, of Freeman stock and she did not consider that a gentleman should, for instance, have shouted conversations down the open hatch to the engine room on the ferry to St Mawes. Fritz always enjoyed catching up on the harbour gossip, but the voice bellowing up from the gloom below deck was not always as careful with its use of language as May might have hoped. She tried to distract the boys, but they were, of course, fascinated by what was going on and Fritz was always one who enjoyed playing to an audience. There were however occasions when even the boys were embarrassed, and Wilf remembered times when he heartily wished that he was somewhere else. A particular danger spot was on the top deck of trolley buses or trams in London, where Fritz would settle himself down next to anyone who he thought looked like an opinionated gentleman, and then ferment an argument which ended, more than once, with a hurried exit from the bus when other people began to take sides. May doted on her boys, as of course did Fritz, but they had different ways of showing their affection, and as the boys grew up they tended to side with their mother when Fritz appeared, at least in May's opinion, to be playing up.

In 1918 the war finally came to an end, and people began to breathe more freely and look to a more hopeful future. May's hopes were particularly high as she discovered that she was once again pregnant, and that this time things seemed to be going better than before. On the 30th January 1919, Brook Villa echoed to the arrival of Paul Anthony James, who proved to be a robust and healthy baby, who somehow imbued the house with a new sense of being a haven from which past spectres could be banished. Jim had a high, wide forehead which was reminiscent of Hubert, and perhaps this especially endeared him to May.

Wilf with baby Jim in 1919

There was a ten-year gap between Wilf and Jim which meant that Wilf was very much the elder brother, who was established at school and had a circle of friends, especially among the boys in the Cox household at Florence Terrace. Fritz's diary of 1920 is the first one to record family life with both children, and January began in a celebratory mood with a photographic session for Wilf and Jim at Opies in Falmouth, but by the 13th Dr Trail was called in because the baby was constipated, which was a condition which always caused Fritz huge anxiety given the detail with which he recorded his own 'motions' in China when he was feeling under the weather. It is understandable after the nightmare of Hubert's illness, that any signs of sickness were dreaded by Fritz and May, but this time the problem was soon solved, and on the 17th 'Baby walked a few steps by himself this evening and cut first tooth in lower jaw'. Towards the end of the month Wilf had started a cold and the diary records that 'baby's motions very loose', giving that all too familiar feeling of the ups and downs of small children, but at a time before general antibiotics, when doctors prescribed what they could, but most of the medicaments given to children were bought over the counter by their parents. Virolax at 9d and Friar's Balsam at 8d were purchased to help with Wilf's cold, and an alarming sounding 'paraffine medicine' costing 3s 5d had been bought for Jim's constipation, and predictably resulted in the 'very loose motions' in the second half of the month. Fritz recorded the baby's development with the precision of an engineer filling in a daily log, and on Jim's first birthday the entry read 'Baby's birthday – one year old. Babs has 7 teeth, 4 on upper and 3 on lower jaw. Can just toddle a little without help. 24 lbs weight, a nice lively boy for his age'. Jim's development probably owed much to Glaxo dried baby milk which Fritz bought in large quantities. His accounts for January show two purchases of Glaxo at 15s a time, representing a startling £15 in today's money.

The age difference between Wilf and Jim meant that Fritz needed to find ways of having time with both boys, but in different ways. The day after Jim's birthday, Fritz booked seats for the pantomime *Goody Two Shoes* to which he took Wilf at the beginning of February, and as the weather improved through March he took

Wilf out on his bicycle to quiet streets to get him used to riding on roads. By the end of March Wilf was joining Fritz on his bike rides, and together they were exploring further afield as well as making regular trips to the cemetery to attend to the family graves. May was also able to get out and about more and invited Wilf's teacher, Miss Eames, to join them on an outing to see *Wild Beasts*, while Fritz stayed in to look after Jim. In the evenings Fritz now played Euchre with Wilf, which brought back memories of the endless card games on the South China Sea, but also underlined that Wilf was growing up. As the boys were getting older, May was able to take Wilf to a lecture at the Polytechnic on the newfangled 'wireless' as well as taking six-year-old Jim out to tea with Mrs Belletti, the wife of the Falmouth photographer, who was developing a garage business for cars as they became more available and fashionable.

A larger house and a growing family meant more expense, and in March Fritz tackled the elusive Alf Cox on the subject of a rise in pay and within a week had confirmation of an increase of a pound a week. The speed with which a pay rise was agreed showed something of the value which the waterworks put on Fritz's work as he became a trusted and reliable member of the staff, and he was the first person to be called in to meet the London directors when they visited Falmouth and needed to be shown round the works. The London end of the company seemed to remain conveniently in shadow, while the Cornish end dealt with the problems and faced out the complaints of the town council, so it was quite an event when 'Messrs Fookes and Bry' arrived from London and were treated to a good dinner and no doubt a comfortable place to stay. Fritz made no record of what was discussed, but the perennial problem of leaks would certainly have been on the agenda, and it was not long before a Mr Hughes arrived from Messrs Clinton of Liverpool. The company apparently specialized in waste detection, and Mr Hughes was described as 'a water expert' who spent the next couple of weeks prowling around Falmouth by night, accompanied by Fritz, listening for leaks with sounding tubes. It must have been a strange and rather sinister sight to see these two men, muffled against the cold weather of December, creeping around the highways and byways, clutching their tubes and frequently standing literally frozen, with ears pricked for sounds of escaping water. The long nights took their toll, but the exercise proved to be a success, and Fritz was rewarded for his extra work by Gerald Cox calling in at Brook Villa and bringing him a bonus payment of £20. In the meantime the US dollar was under pressure, and since Fritz's investments in Hong Kong were linked to the dollar, he noted that the rate of four dollars to the pound at the beginning of January had grown to five dollars by the beginning of February, and reached a high of six and a quarter a week later. The crisis passed soon enough and Fritz looked for more shares to buy, but within the United Kingdom.

Fritz was very conscious that he had a family to support, and sons who needed his attention and encouragement to make the most of whatever opportunities presented themselves. Sport was high on Fritz's list of interests, and it followed that Wilf would take up tennis and join the swimming club, having been expertly coached by Fritz in the waters of Sunny Cove on Gerrans Point. Wilf was, however, not so keen on music, and despite the efforts of his piano teacher, Mrs Hodges, he only made slow progress. Musically things were made worse by his Aunt Doll's enthusiasm as a teacher, and she was never forgiven by Wilf for holding a sharpened pencil under his wrists to make him keep them up while he was playing. The story of Doll and the pencil torture was repeated to later generations, and it was always held against her by Wilf's children.

Now that Jim had arrived safely and was proving to be a very healthy little boy, life at Brook Villa settled down, and the whole family could relax in familiar surroundings, with friends and relatives within easy walking distance, and only too willing to call in for a cup of tea and a chat. Fritz was happy in his work and the family had their own favourite places to visit, with 'Jim's cove' and 'Wilf's beach' for picnics, Sunny Cove for swimming and Mylor for shrimping. Occasionally there were visits from further afield and the neighbours were always especially interested when May's Aunt Winnie appeared on her bicycle. Winnie was an accomplished watercolourist living in St Ives, who knew the local artists as well as members of the Newlyn School, but perhaps kept herself on the fringe of their world, not

Fritz relaxing in his Chinese slippers at
Brook Villa, Falmouth.

least because she wore plus fours and habitually smoked cigars as
she cycled round Cornwall, with her painting equipment strapped
to her back.

The balmy climate of Cornwall contributed to a sense of days
stretching out into the distance, interspersed with moments of
excitement when the distress rockets went off in the night to signal
a ship on the rocks, or Fritz dropped his glasses into the reservoir
and could see them but not reach them because the water was too
deep. Time however, was indeed moving on, and the boys were
growing up and beginning to stretch their wings, ready to leave the
nest.

Chapter 9

JIM and WILF

When Jim was born, the ten-year difference in age between the brothers meant that Wilf could move into the role of being the older brother, and to some extent he could deflect the attention of his parents and aunts onto his younger sibling. Photographs show the brothers exploring on the beach and helping Fritz sail the quay punt, without any obvious signs of the distance which was to develop between them later on in their lives. Inevitably there were the usual family squabbles and Fritz liked to be able to land the family plus aunts on a beach to have a bathe and picnic, while he sailed off in the boat for a bit of quiet fishing. On the whole this worked well, but it is evident from the diary entries that sometimes he came back to the beach to pick up the family, only to find that all had not been peace and light. Even at some distance from the shore he would have been able to tell by May's face that a heavy silence had fallen, and that the journey home was not going to be the contented ending to the day that Fritz might have hoped. As a child, Wilf had been the centre of attention for not only his parents, but a fairly large circle of family and friends. May's aunts doted on him, and for nearly ten years both his parents had been his constant companions, and as Wilf moved into his teens he responded by withdrawing more into himself, and became more resistant to attempts to jolly him out of his moods. His stock reaction was the 'heavy silence' which was something of a Lewis hallmark, and while Fritz would just take himself off to do something interesting somewhere else, May would fret about how to make everything right again, without any immediate signs of success. If nothing else, the teenage moods signalled that it was time for Wilf to leave the nest, and in May 1926 Fritz took him to London to sit the matriculation exams for entry to London University.

Wilf and Jim sailing the quay punt with Fritz.

London would have seemed a very long way from Cornwall, and it is a measure of Fritz's plans for Wilf that he had decided that he should go to the capital for the next step in his education. It is even more significant that the aim was entry to the London School of Economics (LSE), founded by Sydney and Beatrice Webb with the backing of the Fabian Society, with its reputation for high standards and absence of religious influence. Fritz had kept to the Baptist tradition in which he had been brought up, and it seems that Wilf was quite content to attend chapel regularly with the family, although he was beginning to look elsewhere with more than a passing interest in Anglicanism and the Church of England, which meant that a more obvious choice of college in London would have been King's. The LSE had joined the University of London in 1900 and became its Faculty of Economics, with a mascot of the beaver standing for 'foresight, constructiveness and industrious behaviour', which were all notably secular attributes, but would become guiding principles for Wilf for this stage of his life.

Wilf was not yet seventeen when he and Fritz caught the train from Truro on 28th May and arrived at Kate's house in Streatham in time for tea. Fritz had plenty of experience of arriving in new places and knew how confusing it could be, so he had allowed time the next day to explore the city before it was time for the exams to begin. Even so, Wilf was probably not best pleased to be woken at 05.00 to catch a bus to London Bridge as a prelude to walking down Holborn and on to the Embankment. He was always apprehensive when Fritz decided to walk anywhere, because it could mean an endless trail through London without any immediate prospect of arriving anywhere remotely pleasant. The only prospect that was marginally worse was if Fritz decided to take a bus or a tram and start up one of his mischievous conversations with some unsuspecting fellow passenger. On this particular day Fritz was in buoyant mood and encouraged the reluctant Wilf with a new tennis racquet costing 32s 6d, to give him something else to think about apart from the impending test. On the following day, which was Sunday, they went down to Dartford to visit Doll, and on Monday there was an opportunity to see a bit more of London, travelling up to Euston Square to have a look at the university buildings in Gower Street, before taking a bus to Lords to see the Australians finish an innings against Middlesex.

The exams, which were scheduled to take place over four days, began on 1st June and Fritz went with Wilf to South Kensington in time for the start, and then to meet him for lunch at the Science Museum before seeing him back for the afternoon papers. It was the same pattern on the following days, and while Wilf was working away in the exam room, Fritz occupied himself walking around South Kensington and visiting museums. At the end of the week he tidied up at Kate's house, sent off some washing in a parcel to Falmouth, and caught a train with Wilf to Sheffield to spend some time relaxing with Walter and Charles. The pair finally got back to Falmouth on 10th June and life returned more or less to normal, while Wilf waited for his results.

Back at home, Fritz always had one eye on the sea in case there was something interesting happening, and on the weekend of 19th July 1926 he arranged to meet Jim and Wilf on Castle Point to see one of the most spectacular sights in Cornwall for thirty years, when the 'Big Yachts' came to Falmouth to race in what proved to be an exceptionally exciting event.

> Saturday was a memorable day in the history of local yachting, for, thanks to the enterprise displayed by the Royal Cornwall Yacht Club, the big racing cracks visited Falmouth after an interval of over thirty years. To the older generation it revived many happy memories of the days when Falmouth was regularly visited by the big yachts, when the Royal Cornwall Yacht Club received, in turn with other clubs, a challenge cup from the late Queen Victoria and King Edward for competition, and when such well known yachts as *Ibex, Bloodhound, May* and *Satanita*, used to cause much excitement.[1]

By any standards the Big Yachts were enormous – *Shamrock IV* measured 75 feet on the waterline and 110 feet overall – and only

---

[1] *Falmouth Packet*, 19th June 1926.

very rich and powerful people were capable of owning and racing them. A new International Rule was brought into force in 1920 which applied to yachts of up to 14 ½ metres, and by introducing penalties and restrictions on larger boats, had the effect of making big yacht racing less popular with owners. Despite this, the big class did continue and *Britannia* regularly raced with *White Heather* and *Westward,* and it was one of these events which had been brought to Falmouth together with *Shamrock IV.* As Fritz and the boys looked out from Castle Point, they could see all four boats as they prepared to race the triangular course of twenty-one miles which stretched from Falmouth out into the English Channel, and which had to be completed twice to decide the winner for a first prize of £80 with £40 for second place. The spectators on the shore were witnessing a magnificent sight, with four of the most famous yachts of the day competing for the honours. The King's yacht *Britannia* of 221 tons had recently been converted from gaff to Bermuda rig, and was competing with Sir Thomas Lipton's *Shamrock IV* of 175 tons, which had done so well in the 1920s America's Cup against *Resolute.* The third competitor was the famous racing schooner *Westward* of a

The racing schooner *Westward* with every square foot of canvas set.

massive 323 tons, belonging to F T B Davies, and the quartet was completed by Lord Waring's *White Heather* of 179 tons. The start was marked by the committee boat which was, on this occasion, the tug *Joyce Mitchell*, moored off Castle Point in line with St Anthony lighthouse. The watchers on the shore were treated to a quite remarkable sight as the huge vessels competed for advantage in the very confined space at the mouth of the harbour, waiting for the starting signal to be given.

> The start was most exciting. For about a quarter of an hour the yachts manoeuvred around the committee vessel, all carrying their jack yard topsails. On the five minute signal, foresails were hoisted and yachts jockeyed for position. When the starting gun was fired some most thrilling moments were experienced by those on the committee vessel. The *Westward* was nearer to the line and the *White Heather* was a quarter of a length to the rear. The huge schooner seemed to cover the cutter and drive her onto the *Joyce Mitchell*. *White Heather* kept her position and it appeared as if she would smash into the stern of the committee vessel. There were plenty of shouts of warning on each yacht, but there were two men who kept cool; they were the skipper and helmsman of *White Heather*. The skipper was standing amidships and when it looked as if the cutter would strike the committee vessel three feet from the end of the stern an order was shouted and the *White Heather's* course was altered. But there was more excitement in store. To all appearances a collision between Lord Waring's yacht and the *Westward* was inevitable, for it seemed as if the *White Heather* was sailing into a wedge formed between the committee vessel and the schooner. When there seemed no possible chance of preventing a collision, "Luff her" was the command shouted by the skipper, and the yacht immediately answered her helm and headed away from the *Westward*, missing her by inches, much to the relief of those on board the committee vessel. Some idea of the narrow escape from the collision can be gathered from the fact that the *White Heather's* side scraped along the outer belting of the *Joyce*

Mitchell and when she got clear it was seen that she had a long black streak of tar or paint on her otherwise spotless clean white side.[2]

The drama was not lost on Fritz and the boys as they watched the near disaster at very close quarters, as the yachts flew across the bay fighting for whatever advantage they could extract from the course. As it happened, the skipper of *White Heather,* who had judged things so finely at the start, ran too far up under the lea of Gerrans Point in the hope of gaining some benefit from the flood tide, but instead of that he lost the wind. The drop in speed was so sudden, and the boat took so long to recover that Fritz thought that she had gone aground, but in any case the mistake proved fatal to Lord Waring's hopes of winning. The race was eventually won by *Shamrock IV* with *Britannia* second, and *White Heather* very much the last. The race marked a moment in time when the big yachts were beginning to make a come back, though *Westward* was subsequently enlisted for the German Emperor's maritime aspirations, and had her name changed to *Hamburg II*, and in 1936 when King George V died, *Britannia* was scuttled by his order in the English Channel. On a happier and more hopeful note, in 1999 *Shamrock IV's* successor *Shamrock V* was restored and rebuilt at Pendennis Shipyard, where a whole new generation of super yachts are being developed in Falmouth today.

The big yachts were enormous compared with the sailing boats that normally frequented the harbour, and most of the local people who sailed regularly used locally made boats of far more modest proportions. Fritz wrote in some detail about the painting, mooring and storing of his boats, and from photographs it is possible to recognize his main sailing boat as a quay punt although the name *Teal* does not connect with any known boat. He had a smaller sailing boat called *Swallow,* and later he was the proud owner of a motorboat called *Elf.* The boats were kept at Thomas's yard at Ponsharden and were conveniently on Fritz's route to and from work in Penryn. Even Wilf was prevailed upon to do some scraping and

[2] *Falmouth Packet*, 25th June 1926.

painting at the beginning of the season, but since he was not of the same practical bent at Fritz, he was confined to painting bottom boards and bits of the hull that would be safely concealed underwater.

The summer was moving on in Cornwall and it was not just Wilf who was anxious to know the results of his exams. At last the fateful letter dropped onto the front door mat and Wilf learned that he had passed 'Matric' and would be on his way to new things in a few week's time. Fritz had already given both boys a shilling for their school reports, but he now gave Wilf a pound to mark this particularly important moment in taking the next step in his education, which Fritz regarded as of the utmost importance. Fritz had done well in his apprenticeship at Cox's but he wanted something more for his own boys, and part of his financial planning was geared to being ready for what it would cost, and the fact that he would need to take time off work to make sure that Wilf was well settled into his new student life. Nothing was to be left to chance, and on the 2nd October the whole family set off by train to London for what would be nearly three weeks with Kate, while everything was be put in place to make sure that Wilf could be safely left on his own. Kate and John McGill were more than happy to have the family to stay and to save Fritz the cost of board and lodging, but even then, it was very expensive to provide all that was needed for Wilf's new life at university. In 1926 Fritz was earning £28 a month at the waterworks but the train fares to London and travelling around on the tube came to over £13, and the university fees, payable in advance, were £26 8s. Then there was all the equipment that Wilf would need, and Fritz took him shopping to buy everything from a pencil case at 9d to a hot water bottle at 2s, together with a locker at the university which cost 5s and text books which came to over £8. The plan was for Wilf to lodge with Doll in Dartford, so Fritz provided her with £62 to cover board and lodging, and a three-month rail pass into the city centre cost a further £2 14s 3d. Fritz had always given May what he called a 'dress allowance', which was what would probably now be referred to as 'housekeeping'. He now set up a 'dress allowance' for Wilf amounting to £3 5s per month, which was to cover his general living costs, although Fritz also sent him a regular guinea each week.

For the time being Wilf was settled in London, and all the signs were that he enjoyed the course and was happy to be away from home and beginning to launch out in a new environment. However, he had been away for less than a year when something happened which was to change one aspect of his life forever. Some years previously the *Daily Mirror* had introduced a children's column which included the strip cartoon 'Pip, Squeak and Wilfred', which started with Pip as a dog and Squeak as a penguin, who were soon joined by Wilfred, a rabbit found in a turnip field, who it was assumed was their baby! The cast was completed with an elderly penguin called 'Auntie' and a villainous Russian spy with a dog called 'Popski'. Pip and Squeak had a daily series of adventures accompanied by the usual cartoon dialogue with voice balloons, and commentary beneath the pictures. Wilfred, however, spoke only in baby-talk and

Pip, Squeak and Wilfred on the front
cover of the 1923 Annual.

his favourite words, known and repeated by every child in the land, were 'gug' and 'nunc'. Unlikely as it may seem, this caught the imagination, not just of children, but of adults as well, and in 1927 the Wilfredian League of Gugnuncs was founded, with many thousands of fans throughout the country, including the future Queen Elizabeth, the Queen Mother. The Gugnuncs held parties and meetings and even organized an annual rally in the Royal Albert Hall, raising funds for children's hospitals and charities. Members of the League could be identified by a small blue enamel badge bearing a pair of outsize rabbit's ears with the initials W.L.O.G. Given the huge popularity of the cartoon and its nationwide following, it is not hard to imagine the problems that it might create for a somewhat serious young man called Wilfred who was trying to gain acceptance in the student world of LSE. Wilf always maintained that it was May who insisted on a change of name, but the timing suggests that Wilf must have been quite as enthusiastic as his mother in avoiding the inevitable comments and jokes. So it was that Wilfred was consigned to history and from that point onwards Wilf became John, although Fritz never really accepted the change and continued to refer to him as Wilf, or occasionally, as 'Bill'.

London suited John, and LSE provided what he was looking for at the time. He thrived on the discipline of economics and the way that it made him learn to use logic, but he was increasingly conscious that there needed to be something more in his life if he was to feel in any real sense fulfilled. The secular atmosphere of LSE had the unexpected effect of making him think more deeply about what he felt was missing, and he started to question whether the Baptist tradition in which he had grown up was sufficiently sustaining for life in a secular world. He began to read more widely, and in the process he came into contact with the clergy at the parish church in Falmouth, who were able to respond to his questioning and take him deeper into an understanding of himself and his beliefs. Fritz must have been surprised that John's time in a notably secular part of a university should bring him in due course to consider Confirmation in the Church of England, but this was the next step that John took on his journey, and the Bishop of Truro's laying on of hands at the Church of St Charles the Martyr in Falmouth was something that he never forgot. The service marked a very definite moment in time at which John took a decisive step away from the tradition in which his parents and grandparents had been brought up. May had seen it before in the way that her father had changed from being a Baptist minister to becoming an Anglican parish priest, but that change had more to do with exchanging one role for another, while for John, his acceptance into the Church of England was the beginning of seeing his whole life in a new way.

The last of Fritz's diaries to have survived was the one for 1928, so it is not possible to trace how the question of John going on to another university emerged. There is no doubt at all that Fritz felt that a good education was something that he would strive to provide for his boys, but even he must have been a little amazed by the way in which that dream became reality, as both his sons went in due course to Cambridge. However, the dream could only be achieved if Fritz bore the cost, and his income was derived partly from his salary from the waterworks, and partly from the dividends of the share portfolio that he had carefully built up over the years since he had started work. As he contemplated the thought of paying

Jim at Bradfield School

for three years at Cambridge, he was only too conscious of the very slow recovery of the British economy after the First World War. The country had lost about half its merchant shipping fleet to U-boats, and the result had been a huge loss in foreign trade. Things were made worse by the decision in 1925 by the Chancellor, Winston Churchill, to restore the pound to the gold standard at its pre-war exchange rate of US$ 4.86, which immediately slowed recovery and made exports more expensive. The Wall Street crash of October 1929 was the last straw, as most countries around the world suffered in one way or another from the Great Depression for the next three or four years. Fritz was fortunate in having a job and living in the southern half of England, which suffered considerably less than the Midlands and the north because it was much less dependent on the old heavy industries, and was already benefiting from some of the newer industries, like car manufacturing, which had come into the south. Fritz's investments were affected like everyone else's, but he had the advantage of having some of his money in Hong Kong, which was influenced more by what was happening in the East then the West. China, which was on the silver standard rather than the gold, was not nearly as badly affected as countries like Britain and America that had to abandon the gold standard in order to recover. So it was, that despite what was happening in the world at large, Fritz was sufficiently confident to be able to send John to Cambridge, where he took up residence at Gonville and Caius on 1st October 1930, and three years later achieved a 2.2 in History.

As it turned out, John's time at university was not without some friction with his father over money. Fritz was more than ready to carry the cost of the university fees and he had become used to meeting John's costs of board and lodging, but his ever careful nature meant that he was given to scrutinizing John's accounts in very much the same way that he kept an eye on his own. Inevitably there were times when father and son did not see eye to eye, and one particularly fraught example was the matter of grapefruit for breakfast. John liked to start the day with a sustaining cooked breakfast, which Fritz readily understood, but he just could not accept that bacon and eggs with all the trimmings needed to be

John, far right, on the day he received his degree at Cambridge

preceded by grapefruit! May did her best to diffuse the situation, but the argument would not go away and rumbled on through an entire summer vacation.

Cambridge provided opportunities for other things besides food, and it was only a few weeks into his first term that John discovered that rowing in an eight on a river was a rather different experience from rowing in a dinghy on the sea, although both required something of the same skills. At six foot two inches, and weighing twelve and a half stone, John was selected to row at number three in the Caius' Second Boat as one of the workhorses in the crew, and stayed with the boat into his second year. By the time he entered his third year in 1933, his thoughts were beginning to move away from sport towards the possibility of offering for ordination as a priest, and one immediate outcome of that idea was that he became Chapel Clerk. In addition, perhaps because of awareness in the university of the devastating effects of mass unemployment in the early 1930s, he took on responsibility for the

Caius and Trinity Hall Boy's Club, which organized various sporting activities, as well as offering residential camps on the Isle of Wight during vacations. John's grandfather, Arthur, who had died more than ten years before John was born, had always had a particular concern for the children of poorer families and it seems to have come through in John as he walked round the summer camp, in very long black shorts, smoking his ever present pipe and shouting encouragement to the boys. The same thread was picked up again later when he became Head of Oxford House.

The role of Chapel Clerk was perhaps a more obvious indication of the direction of John's thoughts as he began to consider a vocation to the priesthood, and despite his determination not to be diverted from his grapefruit for breakfast, he must have been very conscious that his father had already carried the very considerable cost of his time in London, followed by three years in Cambridge, and that a further period at theological college would be asking a great deal. John applied for, and was awarded, a Steel Studentship under which the university offered a bursary to a graduate who was offering for Holy Orders, which meant that John could go on to Westcott House for theological training, without relying so exclusively on money from his willing but long-suffering father. Westcott was, and is, very much part of Cambridge and the university, and John was able to relax into a different kind of college life, with less emphasis on exams and more on personal reflection and development. The Principal at the time was the famous B K Cunningham, who was given to brief and laconic comments that remained with John as touchstones for life. 'BK' did not like undue fuss, particularly in liturgy, and he had his own ways of curbing the ambitions of the more outlandish students. Asked by one rather precious young man if it would be right to genuflect at a particular point in the service, BK's bored response was 'You can stand on your head, if you know what it means'. It was a throwaway comment, but John treasured it as an example of a wonderfully practical way of cutting through what he saw as ritual for ritual's sake. The experience of LSE had served him surprisingly well in sharpening his sense of practicality, and Westcott then helped him to apply it to his theology, and in the future he was to develop his own laconic responses to over eager clergy.

John was ordained deacon in 1935 and served his title at St Margaret's, Lothbury, before being made priest in 1936 and completing his curacy in the following year. A first curacy was usually followed by a second before someone was considered sufficiently experienced to be given responsibility for their own parish. However, in 1937 John was rather surprisingly asked to become Head of Oxford House in Bethnal Green, an unusual offer to a Cambridge man, and a post of some responsibility for a relatively inexperienced curate. Oxford House was the first university 'settlement', established by Keble College as a house where graduates, tutors and prospective ordinands could live together and experience something of disadvantaged areas at first hand. The members of the house were to offer practical support to local communities as part of an early experiment in community development, and photographs show enthusiastic, pipe-smoking, tweed-jacketed young men, earnestly doing their best in an area of London which was still suffering severely from the Depression. There had been a steady growth in the number of settlements in the early years of the century, but the 1930s saw a very rapid expansion in numbers until they were established in most cities in Britain as well as in Canada and the United States. Arthur would have been delighted by the concept, and perhaps even John would have been surprised if he had known that something that had begun in depressed economic times would continue to flourish. Today, Oxford House provides a café and meeting space for local community use, as well as dance and drama studios and an art gallery. The chapel is carefully preserved as evidence that the original foundation was based on Christian principles, though now the ethos is described as 'value led', which John would probably have accepted as a suitably practical description, given what he had learned from LSE and 'BK'.

The local communities were certainly in need of support and encouragement, particularly now that economic disadvantage was being compounded by the dark threat of war in Europe, with all the hardship that that would bring, and which was a living memory from only twenty years earlier. There was however another, unexpected, dimension to life at Oxford House. John had met Winifred Mary Griffin, who was working as a secretary for the Diocese of London, and who brought a breath of fresh air into what had become a rather stuffy and smoke-filled establishment. The couple had a number of things in common, not least that both their fathers spent their early years at sea, and Mary had also suffered from being called 'Wilfred', due to a garbled message being passed up the dinner table on her first day at a new school. John and Mary were married on 23rd July 1938 in the parish church of Christchurch, Southampton, and Mary moved in with John to enjoy the dubious delights of a male-dominated residence. At the wedding Fritz spent a contented day sharing stories of the sea with Mary's father Cyril, and May gave Mary some prenuptial advice about saving hot water by bathing once a month, and changing her knickers once a fortnight.

Wilf, now called John, marries Mary
Griffin at Christchurch, Southampton,
23rd July 1938.

As Fritz watched the first of his sons getting married his thoughts turned inevitably towards what kind of future they could expect, against the background of rising tension in Europe and the remorseless progress of Hitler in Germany. It was less than twenty years since the end of the nightmare of the First World War and it must have been hard to believe that the world was about to slip into the same abyss once again. Fritz was however a realist, and as he reflected back to his own youth and family life in Norway, he also realized that the time was coming when it would no longer be possible to revisit the country of his early days, and that if he was to see it again then the trip must be soon. He had talked often enough to May about life on the smallholding at Bærum and he wanted her to experience it for herself before it was too late. May had never been abroad before, but she was more than ready to join in the adventure, and they travelled up to Newcastle to board the *MV Black Prince*, a very recently completed passenger and cargo ship of the Fred Olsen Line, bound for Oslo. Fritz had probably picked the ship very carefully as a vessel equipped with the latest air-conditioned ventilation, hot and cold running water in all cabins, and 'numerous baths with hot and cold water (salt and fresh), also a Turkish bath and the most modern appointments for the comfort of passengers'.[3] Fritz was able to have as many baths as he liked in any combination of heat and water, but would have been shocked if he had known that all this luxury would be commandeered by the German Navy within the year, and that the *Black Prince* would end up on fire in the port of Danzig in 1941, and would never put to sea again. For the time being both May and Fritz consigned the spectre of war to the back of their minds and May concentrated on keeping a record of the journey, illustrated with postcards that she pasted into a specially bought new album, but unfortunately without including written details of their itinerary. They travelled between Bergen and Oslo and the journey was illustrated with pictures of comfortable hotel lounges, along with cold, snowy mountains and warmer-looking lakes and chalets. Oslo was a special delight and would have been familiar to Fritz with its fine buildings and sailing boats on open

---

[3] Fred Olsen Line brochure.

water. A visit was paid to the Fram Museum where Nansen's famous boat had been brought and restored a few years earlier in 1935, having been neglected and very nearly lost for ever. The *Fram* was originally commissioned for Nansen's expedition to the Arctic and was designed to withstand the pressure of being frozen into pack ice, with a hull which would allow the boat to rise up and 'float' on top of the ice rather than being locked within it. Electric power for lights was provided by a windmill and the cabin insulation was thick enough to protect a crew for up to five years on board. The *Fram*, meaning 'forward', had a history that would have appealed to Fritz because she was, and still is, the vessel that holds the record for a wooden ship that has sailed the farthest north and farthest south in the world. Although she was originally built for exploration to the North Pole with Nansen, she was later used by Amundsen for an extraordinary expedition which set out for the North Pole, but which was then secretly redirected to the South Pole when Amundsen heard that the Arctic pole had been claimed by Frederick Cook and Robert Peary. Amundsen set off in the *Fram* to reach the North Pole by rounding Cape Horn and heading up to the Bering Strait, so his crew were unaware of any changes until the ship reached Madeira where they were informed of the new plan. Fortunately they were content to go on, and the expedition backers, who learned of the new plans at the same time, were willing to continue their support. It was from Madeira that Amundsen sent his cryptic telegram to Scott, informing him that there was a Norwegian bid for the South Pole.

The trip to Norway brought back many memories for Fritz and it enabled May to see where he had been born and why he was so much in love with the sea and everything connected to it, but it was soon time to leave. The *MV Venus* carried them back to Newcastle and the train took them to Falmouth, with an album full of postcards and an impending sense that the visit had been made just in time.

At the point at which John was starting his new job at Oxford House, Jim was getting ready to go up Cambridge where he had secured a place at Clare to read history. He too found that rowing was a natural sport for a man from Falmouth and was picked to row in Clare's Second Lent Boat in 1938 and then in the First Lent Boat in 1939 when it bumped Jesus to become Head of the River. Jim had started his education at Selwood School in Falmouth and Fritz had then sent him to Bradfield from 1933 to 1937 before he started at Cambridge, where his time was cut short by the outbreak of war. Within two weeks of war being declared Jim joined the Royal Artillery, and it was not long before he was sent to France to provide artillery support for the ill-fated British Expeditionary Force. However, it was not just his higher education that had been interrupted by hostilities. Jim had fallen in love with Jean Louise Standish, and they were married at Selby Abbey on 12th October 1940, only a few months after he had been evacuated from Dunkirk. Photographs show a strikingly handsome couple.

Jim marries Jean Louise Standish in
Selby Abbey, 12th October 1940.

Following the lightning German advance through France and a series of other reversals, Winston Churchill had called for the formation of a highly trained force that could mount surprise attacks along the coast, and as a result, the commando concept was born. Jim was one of the early volunteers and joined No. 6 Commando, which was later combined with No. 5 Commando and became a company-sized element of the 5th Special Service Battalion based at Helensburgh in Scotland. It was during this time that he was involved in training on Loch Linnhe for seaborne landings, and although it could be an unbelievably inhospitable part of Scotland, it held fond memories for Jean who sometimes stayed nearby, and who later requested that her ashes should be scattered on the Linnhe waters in memory of happy times with Jim.

The early commando operations were particularly perilous, and Jim was part of one abortive plan for a raid on the Norwegian coast in December 1941, when No. 6 Commando joined with No. 12 Commando for *Operation Kitbag*. The force eventually had to withdraw, but only after an excruciating time at sea and an on-board explosion that killed six men and seriously wounded eleven others. Experience however, eventually paid off, and the strategic effectiveness of commando units became increasingly apparent. In November 1942 Jim's unit was part of the spearhead force tasked with capturing the harbour at Algiers as part of *Operation Torch*, but most of the landing craft missed the rendezvous with the motor launch that was to guide them into the landing beaches. No. 9 Troop tried to land at Ilôt de la Marine, which was described as 'the most heavily fortified part of Algiers harbour' and it was here that the majority of the commando's casualties were suffered. Of the six boats that were coming in, four were sunk and the officer in command was killed. The citation for the Military Cross awarded to Jim stated that 'Major Lewis took command of the remaining two [boats] and landed. He established communication with his supporting unit and throughout the day passed valuable information and in the afternoon called for F.A.A. [Fleet Air Arm] bomber support which was directly responsible for the capture of Fort Duperre'. News of Jim's MC eventually reached the *Falmouth Packet*, which was able to offer its congratulations to Fritz and May, although the details of exactly what had happened in North Africa could not be made public at that time. There was little rest for No.6 Commando, which was ordered from North Africa to take part in the landings in Sicily marking the beginning of the Italian campaign. Having survived the assault on Algiers unscathed, Jim was unlucky enough to be wounded in Sicily and evacuated to Malta for a spell in hospital before being flown home in a Dakota from Algiers in January 1944. Three months respite followed while he stayed with Jean's parents in Selby where Jean was working with the Land Army and Jim was able to recuperate in the fresh Yorkshire air. It was a relief to be away from the noise and trauma of the fighting for a while and to have time to relax with Jean, and on the 15th December 1944, Penelope Jean was born, although by this time Jim was already back in the thick of it. No. 6 Commando had become part of the 1st Special Service Brigade and been preparing for the D-Day landings. The Brigade's task was to land behind the 8th Infantry Brigade and link up with the 6th Airborne Division on the eastern flank of Sword Beach. Jim had been made troop commander of No.1 Bombardment Unit and had a crucial role in the operation and was Mentioned in Dispatches.

> Major Lewis acting in the capacity of Senior Bombardment Liaison Officer Airborne Division carried out his work afloat showing exemplary devotion to duty.

> The deployment of Forward Observers Bombardment in the Sword area of operation Neptune showed that his planning had been carried out with more than the average care and forethought. The work that descended upon him during the first month of the operation Overlord required and demanded a high degree of concentration and efficiency. Major Lewis not only carried out these duties in an exemplary fashion, but also found time to encourage his Officers and men in their tasks ashore.[4]

---

[4] Lieutenant Colonel Sinclair, Combined Operations Command.

No. 6 Commando continued to fight in the front line for the remainder of the war in Europe until they reached the Baltic Sea and Germany surrendered. Jim was awarded the Africa, Italy, France and Germany Stars, which shows that he was with No.6 Commando all the way, although his service record is yet to be released for this period of the war. There was however an extraordinary coincidence in 1946 when one of May's distant relations, a great grandson of John Freeman of Woodlane, also called John Freeman, bumped into Jim in Malaya, as the war against the Japanese came to an end. He mentioned the meeting in a letter and described Jim as 'an individualist, I have an idea he was with a special unit – possibly SOE'. It was one of those strange random meetings in wartime, but it indicates that Jim was later involved in special duties in another theatre of war.

After his hard and distinguished service during the war, Jim continued in the army in peacetime, but like many others, found it a very different experience. In 1949 he was sent to the Gold Coast, now Ghana, as military advisor to the civilian police, and in 1950 he was seconded to a South Korean Artillery Unit as a liaison officer, where he was seriously wounded but continued at his post, directing fire onto the advancing North Korean forces, eventually forcing them to retire. After this he was medically evacuated to Japan where he spent some time in an American hospital, before returning to England and joining the Royal Army Education Corps attached to 1st Battalion Rifle Brigade before he finally left the Army in 1959 and returned to live in Falmouth.

The war had affected Jim in a number of ways. Despite physical healing, his war wounds and his experiences of battle had left their scars, and the long absences on active service had brought his marriage to Jean to an end, although letters found after she died, showed that she and Jim had continued to keep in touch, and she was able to offer him advice and some comfort in his troubles in later life. In 1952 he married Queenie Passmore and adopted her son, Spencer, who joined the merchant navy and carried on the seafaring tradition that Fritz understood so well. Of Fritz's two sons, it was Jim who maintained a closeness to the sea, with a boat for fishing and running pleasure trips, and walks along Cornish beaches, while John lived some distance away, but regularly came down for summer holidays, and sailed with Jim Morrisson in *Mayflower,* a Falmouth working boat.

By the time that Fritz reached the age of sixty he had accomplished most of what he felt that he needed to do in establishing his family and setting his boys on their ways in life, but there was yet one more crisis to meet and overcome. He had become conscious that the inner energy, which he tended to take for granted, was beginning to disappear. At first he thought it was just one of the effects of getting older, but it slowly began to dawn on him that it was something more, and he reluctantly took himself off to the doctor for a fuller examination. Fritz's surviving diaries do not reach beyond the late 1920s, so the precise cause of his trouble remains a mystery, but it was some sort of cancer that was sapping his strength and it needed urgent treatment. Although antibiotics were a treatment of the future, cancerous growths had been on the receiving end of a considerable amount of research, and Marie Curie's Radium Institute, which had been set up in Paris had been replicated in a large number of major cities throughout the world, including London. In early July 1932, Fritz caught the Cornish Riviera at Truro and travelled up to Streatham to stay with Kate and John McGill at their home at 83 Mount Nod Street. It was fortuitous that Kate was living in London, and could be there once again as a place of refuge and comfort for Fritz, as she had been at other critical moments in his life. On the morning of Monday 4th July, Fritz woke early and wrote to May. The letter was written in pencil on an ordinary sheet of unheaded paper, and since it is the last surviving document penned by Fritz, it can be said to represent his final testament.

My Dear old girl also Bill and Jim,

I think much of you all this morning. It is now 6.30 and I have just read Isaiah 52 and Psalm 23. It is a fine morning and I shall soon be getting up and be on my way to the Radium Institute. I write these lines to let you know that I am thinking of you all.

I rest in the promise of God's Eternal Mercy and trust He will spare us to one another for many years but in case of anything otherwise I want you to know that my thoughts are of you and the Many Happy times we have had. Mourn not for me but remember Hubert and I are together at last with all the dear ones gone before, if ever your eyes see this just realise that Happy memories cling to you all. My dear ones love one another and above all love Him who gave His life for us, so with all Hope I write these few lines and go forth on the Great Adventure either to live or to die.

The treatment at the Radium Institute was crude but successful, and Fritz returned to Falmouth, free of his cancer, and more than ready to get back to his allotment and go fishing in his boats. It had been a close call, but he had come through once again. He lived happily for another eighteen years and died peacefully at Brook Villa in 1950, having seen both his sons through their education and into work and marriage, and four grandchildren safely born. He was buried in the plot in Swanpool cemetery that he had bought for Hubert, at the top of the slope above the Freeman family vault, and not far from his parents' grave. He had come full circle and he could look back on what he would consider a job well done, although it left May without the one man who had filled her life. She followed the Victorian fashion and dressed in black for the rest of her life, although her mourning did not dim her sense of humour or her enjoyment of life. She carried on living at Brook Villa where she liked to be visited by her sons whom she encouraged to come and stay and bring her grandchildren with them. Having young children in the house brought back memories of the early days on Trelawney Road, and her favourite time of the day was the evening when the kitchen table could be cleared of all the supper clutter, and the children would sit round ready for an evening of games with granny. Battered boards and counters were brought out for Reversi and Lotto, and a very worn set of cards was produced for endless games of Rummy and Bezique, and May would hold court and join in the laughter and banter, before it was time for bed. The abiding memory of her grandchildren was her very soft but ample cheeks which they stood on tiptoe to kiss before climbing the stairs to sleep.

When Fritz was in China, May had been careful to send him regular copies of newspapers and magazines so that he could keep in touch with what was happening at home, and now she adapted the idea by asking each of her grandchildren to choose a monthly magazine that she would buy and send to them, tightly rolled up and held together with a label for posting. It appeared to be a complicated and time consuming process, but it meant that May could read the magazines before she sent them off, and that therefore there was always something in common to talk about when everyone met up again in the summer. Her ability to accommodate new ideas was however sometimes tested, as when one of the grandchildren requested a change from *Boy's Own Magazine* to *Practical Wireless Constructor.* May took the alteration in her stride, reading the new magazine in detail and more than ready to have a conversation about how crystal sets could be made at home, and what the bits would cost. Her main concern was that the children should enjoy what they read, and if that was the case then she too was content.

May continued to live at Brook Villa until she was well into her eighties when she moved to Shropshire to be near John and his family. She died in 1965 and her body was carried back to Falmouth to be buried with Fritz and Hubert in the plot at Swanpool cemetery, which had been preserved so carefully for that purpose, and where they could all rest in peace, within sight and sound of the sea.

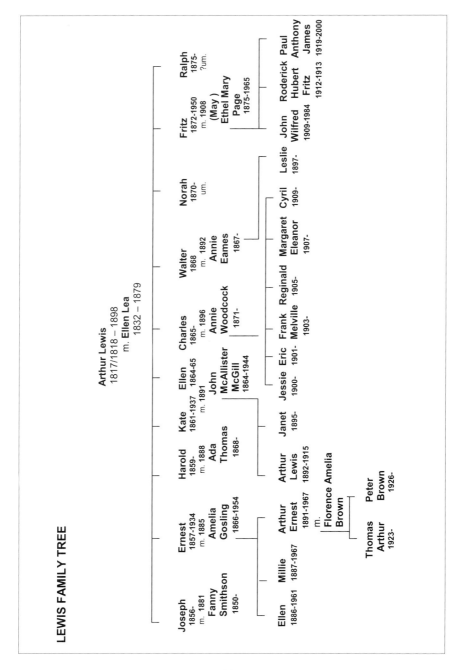

APPENDIX 1

FRITZ'S SHIPS

Ships mentioned in Fritz's diaries:

Ship No.	Name	History	Route
72355	*ROSENEATH*	Built 1875 by Day Summers & Co. of Southampton. 119 gross tonnage. Steam yacht.	Fritz engineer 1897/98 in Med.
102400	*PALAWAN*	4,686 tons passenger ship. Built in 1895 by Caird & Co., Greenock, P&O Far East service. Forty-five first class and forty-four second class cabins. 1914 sold to Indian owners and renamed *Jeddah*. Broken up in Genoa in 1924.	Fritz travelled to China in 1904.
144406	*KLEIST*	8,950 tons cargo/passenger ship Built 1907 by Schichau of Danzig for Norddeutscher (NDL). Sold to the Japanese government in 1921 and became the *Yoshino Maru*. Torpedoed by a submarine 31.07.1944.	Fritz returned from China to Southampton in 1908.
		WEST RIVER	
109874	*TAK HING*	Built by Kwong Hip Loong, Hong Kong named *Kwong Hing*. 617 tons. Sold 1903 HCMSC (1/3), CNC (1/3) and Jardine Matheson (1/3) as *TAK HING* for West River run. 18.09.06. blown ashore at Kowloon in typhoon. 11.06 sold for salvage to Sze Yap SS Co. Ltd. 19.10.09 blown ashore at Kong Moon by typhoon and refloated. 1910 renamed *Hing Lee* and 1912 sold to Wing On SS Co., Ningpo.	Bought by HCMSC to run with *Nanning* and *Sainam* on West River. Did not work out. Sold 1906
116036	*LIN TAN*	572 tons, built by Hong Kong & Whampoa Dock in 1904 for HCMSC for Hong Kong/West River run. Similar in size to *NANNING* and *SAINAM*. 1927 became *Chung On*. Scuttled in Hongkong 8.12.1941.	For Hong Kong + West River to Wuchow
109856	*NANNING*	569 tons. Sternwheeler paddle steamer. Built by G.Fenwick & Co. Ltd, Hong Kong in 1900 for HCMSC. Sold in 1917 to Sai Hing SS Co. Hong Kong.	Canton / West River service to Wuchow
109859	*SAINAM*	Built by G. Fenwick & Co. Ltd, Hong Kong for HCMSC to run with *NANNING*. 588 tons. Mid 1906 – holed and beached near Ling Yang Gorge on Canton/Wuchow voyage. 13.07.06 seized by pirates 50 miles below Samshui. One dead. Dec. 1917 sold to Sai Hing & Co. Hong Kong.	Canton / West River service to Wuchow

	SANUI	Steam lighter ordered by HCMSC to work with *LIN TAN*. Fabricated in UK and assembled by Kwong Hip Loong in Hong Kong for HCMSC.	For Hong Kong + West River to Wuchow
		SOUTH CHINA SEA	
98197	AMARA	Built 1891 by Blumer, North Dock, for Persian Gulf SS Co. Ltd, London. 2,454 tons cargo ship. Sold in 1896 to the Indo-China Steam Navigation Co. 1911 became *Taga Maru*. Wrecked near Ichiyezaki, Wakayama 13.3.25.	
120660	CHIP SHING	Built 1906 by Hall Russell, Aberdeen for Indo-China S.N.Co. Ltd (Jardine, Matheson). 1,984 tons cargo ship. Sold in October 1935 to a Japanese breaker.	
88843	FATSHAN	2,260 tons. Screw steamer built by Ramage & Ferguson Ltd, Leith in 1886 for HCMSC but later shared 5/8th HCMSC and 3/8th CNC. Blown ashore at Hong Kong by typhoon. Later refloated. Broken up in 1933 in China.	Hong Kong to Canton
68528	HANKOW	3,073 tons, built by Inglis of Pointhouse for the CNC. Burnt out alongside quay in Hong Kong 14.10.1906. Hulked up to 1937.	
73451	HONAM	2,364 tons – steel hulled paddle steamer Built by A & J Inglis, Glasgow in 1882 for HCMSC. Replaced *KINSHAN*. Sold in 1925 to Mr Yeung Yuk-Shue of Messrs King Wo (furniture makers) for breaking in Hong Kong in 1925.	Hong Kong to Canton
108353	ICHANG	2,002 tons, built by Scott & Co, Greenock for the CNC. Used on river at Canton as feeder for Blue Funnel steamers. Broken up in Shanghai in 1931.	
9872	KINSHAN	1,994 tons passenger ship, built by HK and Whampoa Docks, Kowloon, for HCMSC. Sunk in 29.12.1942. by gunfire from submarine.	HK/Canton
81318	LAERTES	Built 1880 by Scott & Co., Greenock, for Ocean SS Co. (Alfred Holt) Liverpool. 2,148 tons cargo ship. Sank in collision near Pulau Pisang, Malacca Strait 15.12.17.	Blue Funnel
68409	PEKIN	3,076 tons, built by Inglis of Pointhouse in 1873 for the CNC. ? Sister ship to *ICHANG*. Hulked in 1912.	
108726	POWAN	2,339 tons, built in Glasgow by A Stephen & Sons in 1872 for HCMSC to join *ICHANG* and *HANKOW*. Wrecked on rock Cap Suimun en route from Hong Kong to Canton with the loss of fifty lives.	Hong Kong to Canton.

108399	*SHANSI*	Passenger/cargo ship of 2,002 tons, built in 1898 by Scott & Co, Greenock, for the CNC. Broken up in China in 1930.	Thought to be the coaster on which Fritz served in S. China Sea.
87005	*TAIWAN*	Built 1882 by Scott & Co., Greenock for CNC. 1,734 tons. Sold in May 1905 to Jebson & Co., Hamburg. Wrecked in the Hainan Strait 20.10.1919 when owned by Hachiuma Shokai and called *TAIWAN MARU*.	Thought lost in storm 1908, but survived.
		FALMOUTH	
1115826	*PONUS*	Built in 1902 by Russell, Port Glasgow. 5,077 tons cargo ship/tanker Originally built for Anglo-American Oil Co. Ltd, London and named *KENNEBEC*. New owner Tank Storage, changed name to *PONUS* in 1914. *Ponus* was driven ashore in a gale and caught fire 3rd November 1916 on Gyllyngvase Beach, Falmouth. The wreck attracted much interest. Article in *The Times* and account in *Falmouth Packet* 10.11.1916.	
		NORTH SEA TO NORWAY	
5614875	*MV. BLACK PRINCE*	Passenger ship of 5,039 tons. Built by Akers of Oslo for Fred Olsen under Norwegian flag. Launched 22.12.37. In service in 1938. Commandeered by the German Navy, renamed LOFJORD. On fire in Danzig in 1941. Broken up in 1951 in Faslane.	Fritz and May travelled to Bergen in 1938 for visit to Norway, ending in Oslo.
5537820	*MV. VENUS*	Passenger and mail ship of 5,407 tons, built by Helsingor Vaerft of Elsinore in 1931 for B & N Line Royal Mail Ltd (Bergenske Steamship Co.), operating between Bergen and Newcastle upon Tyne. Entered service 4.06.1931. Broken up at Faslane in 1968.	Fritz and May travelled back to England from their trip to Norway, 1938.

ERNEST LEWIS' SHIPS

Ships on which Ernest Lewis served as First Mate or Captain. Compiled from Lloyd's Captains Registers – Vol 36 1884–1887, Vol 51 1888–1895.

Ernest Lewis

Born – Christiania, Norway 1857. Certificate 011004 Plymouth 1884.

Ship No.	Name	History	Owner
82956	*Yedmandale* Oct 1884	2,205 tons. Built 1884 in South Shields by Readheads. Wrecked on Lombard Rocks near St Nazaire 5.11.1901.	P Hick Jr
83851	*Speedwell* March and Sept 1885	974 tons. Built 1880 by Hodgson Soulsby at Cowpen Quay. Wrecked 12 nm North of Adour Mouth 25.12.1922.	E Handcock, Falmouth
89733	*Carn Marth* Apr, Jun, Oct, Nov 1886 Feb, Jul, Oct 1887	1,687 tons. Built 1884 by Tyne Iron at Willington Quay. Wrecked off Cape La Hague 17.5.1909.	E Handcock, Falmouth
82662	*Marion* Jul, Oct 1888 Jan, May 1889	2,085 tons. Built 1880 by J L Thompson at North Sands. Wrecked at Torre Carbonera, NNE Gibraltar 24.2.1895.	J Gray & Co, Whitby
85904	*Duchess of Cornwall* May, Aug, Oct 1890, Jan, Apr, Jun 1891	1,720 tons. Built 1889 by Gray, W. Hartlepool for S.S.Co. Ltd (Chellew), Falmouth. Torpedoed by a submarine 5nm N Cape Barfleur 11.4.1917.	J & R B Chellew, Falmouth
95456	*Pencalenick* Oct 1892	1,877 tons. Built 1888 by Doxford, Pallion as *Chamois* for Jackson Bros & Cory, London. Changed to *Pencalenick* 1889 by R B Chellew. Wrecked near Klitmoller, Jutland 5.3.1933 and broken up at Gothenburg 5.1933.	R B Chellew, Falmouth
99156	*Pendarves* Dec 1892 Jun 1893	2,669 tons. Built 1892 by Dixon (Raylton), Middlesbrough. Broken up at Spezia 17.5.1951.	S.S.Co. Ltd (Chellew), Falmouth
95907	*Penwith* Mar 1893	1,978 tons. Built 1890 by Harvey's of Hayle. Abandoned 45.00N/11.00W 28.12.1911.	S.S.Co. Ltd (Chellew), Falmouth
96638	*Etherley* Apr, Aug 1894 Jan, Mar, May 1895	1,785 tons. Built 1889 by Tyne Iron at Willington Quay. Torpedoed 20nm SE Armen Rocks, 19.1.1917.	Hunting & Pattison, London

HAROLD LEWIS' SHIPS

Harold's career at sea has been difficult to trace. He appears on the crew lists of the two ships below, and he is recorded in the census as a 'Second Mate'.

Ship No.	Name	History	Owner
85806	*Llandaff City*	1,902 tons. Built by Richardson Duck of Thornaby. Launched 1882. Broken up in Genoa in 1922.	Charles Hill and Sons of Bristol. Bristol City Line
91064	*Exeter City*	2,140 tons. Built by Blyth S B of Cowpen Quay in 1887. Broken up in Genoa in 1925.	Charles Hill and Sons of Bristol

APPENDIX 2

GAMES

EUCHRE

Seamen have always used games to pass the time when they are not required to work and some games have found their way around the world by being passed from one crew to another. Fritz mentions a number of games in his diaries and some, like *Euchre*, are found in places with a strong naval connection. *Euchre*, which was derived from earlier card games played in Europe, was modernized in the Napoleonic era and introduced to America around New Orleans from where it spread along the Mississippi River to the Northern States. *Whist* was fading in popularity and *Poker* was more common in the Old West and on riverboats. *Euchre* is a plain five-card trick game for four players. A pack of twenty-five cards is used consisting of the A K Q J 10 9 in each of the four suits plus a joker. Each player is dealt five cards and the next card is turned face up. Players then bid, as in *Whist*, for the number of tricks that they think they can make as well as for which suit will be trumps. The joker, which was introduced into the playing card pack in the 1850s for this particular game, counts as the highest trump and is called the 'Benny' or the 'Best Bower'. The aim is to win at least three of the five tricks, with an extra bonus for winning all five. *Euchre* was eventually eclipsed by *Bridge*, although it has now made a comeback especially via the Internet, and has a huge following in the Mid Western and Northern states.

HEARTS

Hearts is usually played by four people using a full fifty-two card pack. There are no trumps but each heart is worth one penalty point and the queen of spades is worth thirteen penalty points. The game follows the *Whist* pattern but the aim is to score as few points as possible, and therefore to lose tricks rather than win them! On the first hand, before a card is played, each player passes three cards to the neighbour on their left. On the second hand, cards go to the right. On the third hand the cards go across to the player opposite and on the fourth hand no cards are passed at all. The player with the ten of clubs leads for the first trick. The game continues until a player reaches 100 points, when the lowest scorer becomes the winner. The game became hugely popular among children in the nineteenth century, and has taken a new lease of life on the Internet with a US National Championship.

MATADOR

Matador is a Spanish game, whose name literally means 'killing', and is normally played with a standard set of double-six dominoes, twenty-eight tiles in all. Dominoes are played so that the spots on touching ends add up to seven, and the winner is the person who plays all their dominoes to the layout. The 0-0, 1-6, 2-5, and 3-4 are the matadors and can be played on any free end, but the person adding the next domino to a matador must play so that the ends add up to seven as usual (or play another matador). If there is a blank at either end of the layout the only dominoes that can be played there are the matadors. Matadors can be placed in line or across the line, and when laid across, the next player can use either end of the matador to continue the line. At the end of a hand, each player adds up the total number of pips in their hand and the lowest scoring player is the winner.

APPENDIX 3

MEDICAMENTS

Before the days of antibiotics people relied on a number of remedies that could be bought over the counter to treat various ailments or injuries. The family doctor was occasionally able to prescribe a medicine, but Fritz's diaries show that the most usual medical advice was to go and purchase a particular proprietary brand, or a readily available chemical compound. The most common problem for Fritz when he was in China, as well as for his family when he settled in Falmouth, was either too much or too little movement of the bowels. Since medication, like castor oil, was fairly brutal, periods of constipation were usually followed by diarrhoea which then required something to help stem the flow. Apart from stomach upsets, the next most common problems were colds and sore throats. The following is a list of the medicaments mentioned by Fritz in his diaries:

Boracic acid came in the form of crystals that could be dissolved in water and used as a mild antiseptic. It was used particularly for bathing eyes, although more recent advice warns against overuse, particularly with babies and small children.

Camphor oil was used as a chest rub and to relieve the effects of colds. Fritz used it as a moth repellent, and since its fumes are a rust preventative, it was used in tool boxes to protect steel tools.

Castor oil seems to have been used fairly liberally, particularly to deal with constipation, although the level of dosage often seems to have produced an overreaction which then required something to stem the flow. Fritz also gave castor oil to one of his hens when it was not feeling well, with beneficial results.

Cascara tablets were a mild laxative and sometimes used for headaches. Cascara sagrada ('sacred bark') came from the Californian buckthorn tree which was known in the local indigenous dialect as the chittam stick, ('laxative tree') from which the English word 'shit' is apparently derived.

Chlorodyne was a chloroform and morphine tincture that Fritz used in China when he was suffering from a fever, and was usually washed down with a liberal amount of brandy. Not surprisingly, the effect was to produce a deep sleep which was often enough to produce relief from the symptoms, although it sometimes seems to have required more than one further dose.

Eno's salts were the most common remedy for constipation.

Formalin paste was used to treat chilblains.

Formamint tablets were bought from the chemist to treat sore throats.

Friars Balsam was used as an inhalant to help clear a blocked nose.

Ginger was taken in tea to help cure diarrhoea.

Glaxo was the trade name for the dried milk supplement which Fritz bought in large quantities to build up his children when they were very young, and represented a very considerable expenditure.

Kincher salts were purchased and a dose taken, but it was not clear what they were intended to remedy.

Lime Water was a saturated solution of calcium hydroxide (quicklime) which was both astringent and antacid. It was used as a remedy for vomiting and the accompanying nausea, and was added to milk for babies to counteract diarrhoea. Fritz administered it to Jim, as a baby, on the day after he had dosed him with castor oil!

Quinine salts (quinine sulphate tablets) were taken by Fritz when he had a bad stomach ache. The tablets were originally intended as a treatment for malaria, and were later used to treat nocturnal leg cramps, but they would have been a very powerful and uncertain treatment for the digestion. Presumably the tablets were left over from Fritz's time in China and he thought they would at least give him some relief.

Salycilate of soda was a powerful agent in reducing temperature and also relieving pain. It was used for skin conditions such as eczema and was recommended for treating rheumatism in horses! By 1911 the salycilates were superseded by the invention of aspirin.

Virolax cost 9d in 1921 and was advertised as a 'nutrient laxative' which would lubricate rather than irritate the internal tissues, and would 're-educate the intestine to act naturally'.

BIBLIOGRAPHY & SOURCES

Arnold, Julius, *Handbook of the West River,* Hong Kong, Canton & Macao Steamboat Company, 1909.

Arnold, Julius, *Scenery of the West River,* Hood, 1910.

Barnicoat, David, *Sailing Ship to Super Liner, Falmouth Docks 1860–2010,* Seaman Publications, 2010.

Batchelor, Peter F., and Matson, Christopher, *The Western Front 1915,* Sutton Publishing, 1997.

Beauclerk, Lady Di, *Summer and Winter in Norway,* John Murray, London, 1868.

Bird, Sheila, *Bygone Falmouth,* Phillimore & Co. Ltd, 1985.

Blue, Archibald Duncan, *The China Coast: A Study of British Shipping in Chinese Waters 1842– 1914,* Ph.D. Thesis submitted to the University of Strathclyde, 1982.

Brown, Malcom, *The Imperial War Museum Book of the Western Front,* Sidgwick & Jackson, London, 1993.

Burton, Anthony, *Richard Trevithick, Giant of Steam,* Aurum Press Ltd, 2000.

Compton, Nic, *The Great Classic Yacht Revival,* Mitchell Beazley, an imprint of Octopus Publishing Group Limited, 2004.

Conner, Patrick, *The Hongs of Canton, Western Merchants in South China 1700–1900,* English Art Books, 2009.

Darling-Finan, Nicola, *Images of Bygone Falmouth,* Breedon Books, Derby, 2001.

Davies, Alun, *The History of the Falmouth Working Boats,* Troutbeck Press, Mabe 1989, revised and reprinted 1995.

Dick, H.W. and Kentwell, S.A. *Beancaker to Boxboat,* Nautical Association of Australia Inc. (1988). 17 Parer St, Scullin, ACT 2614 Australia.

Drage, C., *TAIKOO,* Constable & Co. Ltd, London (1970).

Ellis, John and Cox, Michael, *The World War 1 Databook,* Aurum Press, 1993.

Falls, Cyril, *The First World War,* Longmans, 1960.

Farr, Grahame, *West Country Passenger Steamers,* T. Stephenson

Fereday, L.A., *The Story of Falmouth Baptists,* The Carey Kingsgate Press Ltd, London, 1950.

Fox, Caroline and Monk, Wendy, *The Journals of Caroline Fox 1835–1871; a selection,* Elek, 1972.

Freeman, *Cornish Granite, Its History, Legends and Modern Uses,* Messrs. John Freeman, Sons and Co. Ltd, Penryn, undated (early 1900s)

Gay, S.E. *Old Falmouth,* Headley Bros.,1903.

Gilson, Peter, *Falmouth in Old Photographs,* Alan Sutton Publishing, 1990.

Guinness, Jonathan, *The House of Mitford,* Hutchinson & Co, 1984.

Haines, G, *Gunboats on the Great River*, 1976.

Haws, Duncan, *Merchant Fleets in Profile*, Patrick Stephens Limited, Cambridge, 1978.

Haws, Duncan, *Merchant Fleets 39, China Navigation Company*, T C L Publications, 2001.

Heaton, Peter, *A History of Yachting in Pictures*, Tom Stacey Ltd, 1972.

Hickman, Katie, *Daughters of Britannia*, Harper Collins, 1999.

Hong Kong, Canton & Macao Steamboat Company, *Handbook* (and maps) printed in Hon Kong by HK&MSCo. 18 Bank Buildings, Queens Road Central, Hong Kong,-1900

Hyde, F.E, *Blue Funnel, A History of Alfred Holt & Co. of Liverpool 1865–1914*

Liverpool University Press, 1956.

Hyde, F.E., *Far Eastern Trade 1860–1914*, Harper & Row, 1973.

Hyde, F.E., *Shipping Enterprise & Management 1830–1939*, Liverpool University Press, 1967.

Howard, David and Howard, Stephen, *The Story of P & O*, George Weidenfeld & Nicholson Ltd, 1994.

Hutton, Will, *The Writing on the Wall – China and the West in the 21st Century*, Little Brown Book Group, 2007.

Johnston, Ian and McAuley, Rob, *The Battleships*, Channel 4 Books, 2000.

Keswick, Maggie and Weatherall, Clara, *The Thistle and the Jade, A celebration of 175 years of Jardine Matheson & Co*, Frances Lincoln Publishers, 1982.

Ke-wen, Wang, Ed. *Modern China, An Encyclopedia of History, Culture & Nationalism*, Garland Publishing Inc., 1998.

Lambert, Andrew, *Battleships in Transition, The Creation of the Steam Battlefleet 1815–1860*, Conway Maritime Press Ltd, 1984. Published by Naval Institute Press for USA and Canada.

Latourett, Kenneth S., *A History of Christian Missions in China*, Macmillan, New York, 1929.

Legge, Rev. Dr, *Three Weeks on the West River of Canton*, compiled from the Journals of Rev. Dr Legge, Dr Palmer and Mr Tsang Kwei-Hwan, printed by De Souza & Co., Hong Kong, 1866.

Marchant, L.R., *Guide to the Archives and Records of Protestant Christian Missions from the British Isles to China 1796–1914*.

Marsden, Philip, *The Levelling Sea*, Harper Press, 2011.

Marriner, S, and Hyde, F.E., *The Senior: John Samuel Swire 1825–1898*. Liverpool University Press, 1967.

Mitchell, Liz and Sexton, Diane, *A Little Book of Big Cornish Achievements*, Atmosphere, Willis Vean, Mullion, Cornwall, 2007.

Milligan, Edward H., *The Biographical Dictionary of British Quakers in Commerce and Industry 1775–1920*, Sessions Book Trust, York, 2007.

Moise, Edwin, *Modern China*, Longman, 1986.

Monk, Wendy, *The Journals of Caroline Fox 1835–1871*, Elek Books Ltd, London, 1972.

Morison, Stanley, *The English Newspaper 1622–1932*, Cambridge University Press, 1932.

Nordstrom, Byron J., *Scandinavia since 1500*, University of Minnesota Press, Minneapolis and London, 2000.

Olver, Edwin T., *The Cornish Riviera, Falmouth and Its Surroundings, A Pictorial Guide and Social Souvenir for 1914–15, 1914.*

Payton, Philip, *Cornwall, A History*, Cornwall Editions Limited, 2004.

Payton, Philip, *The Cornish Overseas*, , Ian Grant, Cornwall Editions Limited, 2005.

Payton, Philip, *Cornish Studies*, Second Series, University of Exeter Press, 2010.

Pollock, John, *Falmouth For Instructions*, Published by J B Pollock.

Reed, Paul, *YPRES – Walking the Salient*, Leo Cooper – Imprint of Sword Books Company, 1999.

Richards, Pamela, *A Quaker Record of Maritime Falmouth in World War One*, Reprinted in *Troze*, the journal of the National Maritime Museum, Falmouth.

Ritchie, L.A., Ed., *The Shipbuilding Industry, A Guide to Historical Records*, Manchester University Press, 1992.

Robinson, Douglas R. R., *Bar Pool*, D R R Robinson, Truro, 1992.

Sainsbury, Maria Tuke, *Henry Scott Tuke, A Memoir*, Martin Secker, 1933.

Spence, Jonathan, *The Search for Modern China*, Hutchinson, London, 1990.

Spencer, William, *Army Service Records of the First World War*, Public Records Office, 2001.

Stanier, Peter, *South West Granite*, Cornish Hillside Publications, 1999

Starkey, David J.,Ed., *Shipping Movements in the Ports of the United Kingdom 1871–1913*, Exeter University Press, 1999.

Starkey, David J., and Jamieson, Alan G., Eds., *Exploiting the Sea: Aspects of Britain's Maritime Economy since 1870*, University of Exeter Press, 1998.

Strachey, Lytton, *Eminent Victorians*, Chatto & Windus, 1918.

Studwell, Joe, *The China Dream: The Elusive Quest for the Greatest Untapped Market on Earth*, London, Profile Books, 2005.

Swallow, Geoffrey, *Imagining the Swimming: Discourses of Modernity, Identity and Nationhood in Annual Swimming Matches in Late Victorian Cornwall*, Cornish Studies, Second Series, 2010.

Thomas, R.D., *Pastures New in a Sternwheeler up the Si Kiang: A Trip on the West River from Canton to Wuchow and Return*, China Baptist Publication Society, 1903. Reprinted by Ch'eng-wen Publishing Co. Taiwan, 1971.

Tremewan, Peter, *The Relief of Poverty in Cornwall 1780–1881* in *Cornish Studies 16*, 2008.

Vernon Gibbs, Commander C.R., *British Passenger Liners of the Five Oceans*, Putnam, 1963.

Warn, W., *Directory and Guide for Falmouth and Penryn*, 1864.

Whetter Dr James, *The History of Falmouth*, first published 1981, revised edition by Lyfrow Trelyspen, The Roseland Institute, Gorran, 2004.

Wilson, David G., *Falmouth Haven, The Maritime History of a Great West Country Port*, Tempus Publishing, 2007.

Younghusband, Colonel, *The British Invasion of Tibet: Colonel Younghusband 1904*, London Stationery Office, 1904.

Other sources:

General Board of Health, *Report to the General Board of Health on Preliminary Enquiries into sewerage, drainage and supply of water and sanitary conditions of the inhabitants of the Borough and Parish of Falmouth*, by Robert Rawlinson Esq., 1854.

Imperial Maritime Customs, China, *Decennial Report on the trade, navigation, industries of ports open to foreign commerce in China and Corea, 1882-9.*

Maritime Customs. 111, Special series 6, *List of the Lighthouses, Light Vessels, Buoys, and Beacons on the Coast and Rivers of China 1907.*

Urban Sanitary Authority, Falmouth.

Report and Valuation of the Gas and Water Works, by Mr Silverthorne, 1896.

Report on the Falmouth Water Supply, Prof. J A Wanklyn, 1897.

-Engineers Report, Proposed Municipal Waterworks Purchase, Falmouth Corporation, 1899.

Report on the Water Supply of Falmouth, Arthur F Phillips, 1900.

Report of the Inquiry by J M Herbert and T Page relating to the proposed Falmouth Waterworks Bill, 1847. Minutes of Evidence.

Annual Report of the Harbour Master of Hong Kong, 1906.

Personal notes made by Mr Abraham and entrusted to Mrs Margaret Powell of Trewoofe, Lamorna, for publication. Mr Abraham started work for John Freeman & Sons in the Penryn office in 1912, working his way up the firm to become company secretary before leaving the firm in 1948. In the 1950s he was Secretary of the Cornish and Devon Granite Masters' Association.

INDEX

The index covers Chapters 1 to 9 of the book but does not cover: Contents, Introduction, Acknowledgements, Dedication, Appendices, Bibliography and Sources, and footnotes. Index entries refer to page numbers. Illustrations are in *italics*. Main subjects in the book have an extra sub-heading for 'passing mentions'. Entries are in letter-by-letter alphabetical order.

SAMPANS AND SAFFRON CAKE